COLUMBIA STUDIES
IN ECONOMICS

5

CONSUMER DEMAND

CONSUMER DEMAND

A NEW APPROACH

Kelvin Lancaster

COLUMBIA UNIVERSITY PRESS

NEW YORK & LONDON   1971

Kelvin Lancaster is Chairman of the Department of Economics at Columbia University.

Copyright © 1971 Columbia University Press
Library of Congress Catalog Card Number: 75-173984
ISBN: 0-231-03357-5
Printed in the United States of America

ACKNOWLEDGMENTS

The author wishes to acknowledge the assistance of the National Science Foundation and the Ford Foundation in supporting the research from which this book has emerged.

Portions of the analysis given here have been published in the *Journal of Political Economy*, *American Economic Review* (*Supplement*), and *Essays in Honour of Lord Robbins*, to be published by Weidenfeld and Nicolson, Limited.

CONTENTS

CONSUMER DEMAND

CHAPTER 1

INTRODUCTION

1.1 Input and Output of Economic Theory

The output, and thus the predictive power and analytical usefulness, of any scientific theory is ultimately limited by the input into that theory. At the same time good theory should be efficient, in the sense that it should not use more informational input for given predictive output than the minimum necessary.

Good theory should be as universal as possible. But universality can easily be misinterpreted. While a prediction that almost anything might happen is universal enough, it is the product of an empty theory unless the circumstances under which each of the possible outcomes will occur are specified. Good theory, in other words, should provide predictive output which is responsive to variation in its informational input.

The accepted theory of consumer behavior in economics is the result of a long process of eliminating excess input and making the theory efficient. The excess input was initially on the psychological side, and relatively strong assumptions about utility and the nature of human psychology were gradually shaved away until it was shown that the predictions of the theory required only weak assumptions about the existence of consistent preference ordering by individuals.

The long concentration on the preference side of consumer demand theory has diverted attention away from the simple fact that demand theory involves two types of input—information about things as well as about people. As it stands in the generally accepted form, demand theory makes no use of information about things. Whereas current theory enables us to trace the effects of different preferences (greater or lesser convexity of indifference curve for example) on demand, it provides no way at all of tracing the effect of changes in the physical properties of goods on demand.

Someone with no economic background, studying the economist's theory of demand, might well find the concentration on preferences, to the exclusion of properties of goods, a strange one. After all, one would expect information on the properties of goods to be more easily obtainable, and to be more universal in character, than properties of individual's preference orderings. A theory that takes no account of information that is readily available, and depends entirely on information that may be available in principle (preference orderings) but not in practice, is surely a strange one.

All economics textbooks use examples which draw upon common sense knowledge of the relationship between properties of goods—that butter and margarine will be closer substitutes than butter and sugar, that the demand for gasoline will not depend much on the price of tea, and so on. But the actual demand theory set out in those books provides no warrant for statements of this kind and no necessary expectation that goods which are close substitutes in the eyes of one person will also be close substitutes to others.

The analysis of this book originated from the simple observation that traditional demand theory was ignoring highly pertinent and obvious information, the properties of goods themselves.

1.2   Traditional Demand Theory

What we shall refer to as "traditional" demand theory is the analysis of consumer choice under budget constraint and the consequent prediction of the change in a consumer's chosen collection of goods when prices change. It is derived from the analysis of Slutsky[1] through the medium of Hicks[2] and has been mathematically refined (but not basically changed) to the state represented in, for example, the work of

[1] E. E. Slutsky, "On the budget of the consumer," 1915, reprinted in *Readings in Price Theory* (American Economic Association), Irwin, 1952.
[2] J. R. Hicks, *Value and Capital*, (2nd. Ed.), Oxford, 1946.

Debreu.[3] Although there is a neo-Marshallian school (represented by Friedman)[4] that makes somewhat different assumptions about just what is supposed to be constant when we trace out a demand curve, all contemporary discussions of the theory of consumer behavior are variants of the basic Slutsky-Hicks analysis.

In this analysis we commence with the complete ordering by the consumer of all possible collections of goods. For the usual simplified two-good version of the analysis, we assume at the outset that if we

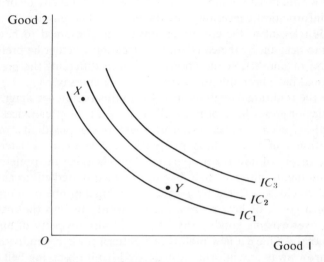

Figure 1.1. Traditional preference map

show diagrammatically all possible goods collections (assuming goods cannot be obtained in negative quantities), then, as between any two collections such as X, Y in Figure 1.1, the consumer has one of the following attitudes: (a) Prefers X to Y (XPY). (b) Prefers Y to X (YPX). (c) Prefers neither X to Y nor Y to X, that is, is indifferent to the choice between X and Y ($X\bar{P}Y$ and $Y\bar{P}X$ or XIY).

We then draw indifference curves covering the whole diagram, each of which joins all collections which stand in an indifference relationship for this particular consumer. If all goods are positively desired (the consumer always prefers a collection with more of any good and no less of any other), all points on an indifference curve which is further from

[3] G. Debreu, *Theory of Value*, Wiley, 1959.
[4] M. Friedman, *Price Theory, a Provisional Text*, Aldine, 1962.

the origin will be preferred to any point on an indifference curve closer to the origin, while considerations of consistency (transitivity) will ensure that no two indifference curves intersect. The shape of the indifference curves (convex toward the origin) can be regarded as an assumption, a reasonable statement of psychology, or as derived from the observation that consumers normally purchase more than one good.[5] The result is the traditional "indifference map" or preference diagram of Figure 1.1.

Once we are given the preference map, we have already incorporated all the information concerning goods as such. The physical properties of goods relevant to the consumer have been presumed to have been taken into account by the consumer in deciding whether he prefers one collection or another. If the goods had been different, the preference map would have been different; that is all we can say.

Since the traditional analysis starts with this preference diagram, the properties of goods have been swallowed up in the preferences before the analysis even commences, and there is no possibility of using information concerning these properties anywhere in a later stage. With no theory of how the properties of goods affect the preferences at the beginning, traditional analysis can provide no predictions as to how demand would be affected by a specified change in one or more properties of a good, or how a "new" good would fit into the preference pattern over existing goods. Any change in any property of any good implies that we have a new preference pattern for every individual: we must throw away any information derived from observing behavior in the previous situation and begin again from scratch. Once the information concerning preferences is fed into the system, the traditional analysis proceeds to superimpose the budget constraint (*AB* in Figure 1.2) on the preference map, finding the consumer's preferred collection subject to the budget constraint at the point on the budget line (*C* in Figure 1.2) where an indifference curve is tangent.

Demand theory is then a comparison of preferred collections under specified changes in the budget. The one certain prediction of the theory is that a change in the price of one good, only, accompanied by a change in income (if necessary) that will either (a) maintain the consumer on his original indifference curve[6] or (b) enable the consumer to

[5] See, for example, K. J. Lancaster, *Introduction to Modern Microeconomics*, Rand McNally, 1969, pp. 162–63.

[6] The Slutsky-Hicks analysis.

buy his original collection (at the new prices) with nothing over,[7] will result in an inverse change in the quantity bought of the good whose price has changed. This effect is the *pure substitution effect*.

The properties of the standard demand curve (effect of a change in the price of one good when *money income*, rather than the level of

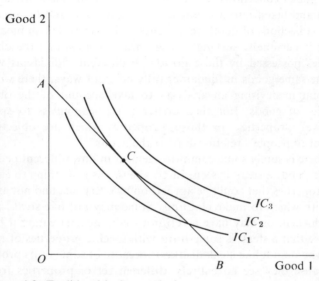

Figure 1.2. Traditional budget analysis

preference, is held constant) are then derived by breaking the adjustment process into two (hypothetical) stages:

(1) The price change, accompanied by an income adjustment to maintain the preference level, giving a pure substitution effect.

(2) A restoration of the money income to its original level. Since the new prices rule, this is a *pure income effect*, equivalent to changing money income with prices held constant.

The prediction of traditional demand theory is confined to the sign of the pure substitution effect. The income effect may be in any direction and depends entirely on the preference map.

[7] The "overcompensation" analysis. See P. A. Samuelson, "Consumption theory in terms of overcompensation rather than indifference comparisons," in Stiglitz (ed.), *Collected Scientific Papers of Paul Samuelson*, MIT Press, 1966.

1.3   Giving Goods Their Due

It is clear enough from the comments on traditional demand theory that we cannot utilize information concerning the known properties of goods unless we commence our analysis at an earlier stage than in the traditional case. Once we have an individual's preferences among various goods collections, the properties of goods have already been weighed and taken into account by the individual, and his preference map on collections of goods represents an inextricable combination of what he is personally seeking in the various goods, and the objective properties possessed by those goods. If different individuals were to "see" the same goods in fundamentally different ways, there would be little point in devising an analysis to take account of the objective properties of goods. For then either it is meaningless to speak of "objective" properties, or those properties which are objective are irrelevant to people's relationship to the goods.

But there is surely some common element in how different people see the same good: a steak is seen, in this sense, as something to eat, with many properties that could be agreed on by everyone, and not as something with which to make clothing. Some may not like steak, or may prefer chicken, or may have a religious tabu against eating it but can still agree that a steak is something with specific properties of its own. Those who do not like steak dislike it because of some of its properties, not because they see an entirely different set of properties from the steak-eaters.

Sometimes, among the many properties of a good, some may be relevant to one individual, others to a different individual. One person may scarcely notice the existence of properties which to him are of little account in his decisions but are important to someone else. A difference in interest and emphasis may lead to differences in the importance of various properties to different people, but if the properties are objective all will agree on them.

Any good possesses an enormous number of physical properties: size, shape, color, smell, chemical composition, ability to perform any one of a variety of functions, and so on. Because not all properties will be relevant to choice, we shall henceforth use the term *characteristics* for those objective properties of things that are relevant to choice by people.

The fundamental propositions on which the analysis of this book is based are two:

(1) All goods possess objective characteristics relevant to the choices which people make among different collections of goods. The relationship between a given quantity of a good (or a collection of goods) and the characteristics which it possesses is essentially a technical relationship, depending on the objective properties of the goods and, sometimes, a context of technological "know-how" as to what the goods can do, and how.

(2) Individuals differ in their *reactions to* different characteristics, rather than in their assessment of the characteristics content of various goods collections.[8] It is the *characteristics* in which consumers are interested. They possess preferences for collections of characteristics, and preferences for goods are *indirect* or *derived* in the sense that goods are required only in order to produce the characteristics. The view of some economists of an earlier generation (Menger, for example)[9] that goods were desired in order to satisfy "wants" was somewhat along the general line of our analysis: the various characteristics can be viewed, if you like, as each helping to satisfy some kind of "want." Generally speaking, it seems better to avoid explicit psychologizing and simply note that it is the characteristics of goods, not the goods themselves, in which people are interested.

Using these two basic propositions, we view the relationship between people and things as at least a two-stage affair. It is composed of the relationship between things and their characteristics (objective and technical) and the relationship between characteristics and people (personal, involving individual preferences).

A variety of models might be constructed on the basis of this two-stage division. The emphasis in this book is on the goods-characteristics relationship, and it is the various possibilities inherent in this that will be developed. For most of the analysis we shall assume that the

[8] This is the working hypothesis of the book. It is clearly not applicable to all cases. People may sometimes appear to "see" properties of a good that are not seen by others and defy objective analysis. Our interest here is in the addition to both analytical understanding and potential predictive power of cases in which the characteristics approach seems to fit. At worst, we fall back on the traditional analysis by assuming that the consumption technology is unknown in practice for some groups of goods.

[9] Karl Menger, *Principles of Economics*, 1950 (English translation).

characteristics-people relationship is of the same kind as the goods-people relationship assumed in traditional theory, that is, that people have well-defined preferences for collections of characteristics, expressible in terms of preference maps with indifference curves convex toward the origin. We shall, however, see that some aspects of preference relationships, such as satiation phenomena, call for more detailed analysis than is given in the traditional case.

1.4   Why?

The omission in the traditional analysis of any provision for using information concerning the technical characteristics of goods renders it completely incapable of handling the most important aspects of demand in an advanced consumer society—the effects of product variations and differentiates, model changes, new goods, and new variants of existing goods.

Suppose that a certain good is changed somewhat in terms of its characteristics. In the traditional analysis, we can do only one of two things: (i) ignore the changes, and proceed as if the new variant is the same good as before or (ii) regard the variant as an entirely new good, throwing out any information concerning demand behavior with respect to the original variant, and start from scratch. The first of these ignores relevant information and will predict unchanged demand where demand conditions have very probably changed. The second throws away previously gathered information that is likely to be relevant and gives us nothing in its place.

In practice, of course, we use our common sense to tell us that a variation in an existing good which leaves the basic function of the goods more or less unchanged, but changes it in some minor way, will cause some change in demand conditions, but not very much. This intuitive expectation is not, however, derived from any properties of traditional demand theory but from the fact that we keep some kind of a characteristics approach in the back of our mind, whatever the formal theory may be.

Traditional demand theory, like the traditional theory of the firm, has its roots in the economics of an earlier, and simpler, society, when there were fewer products, each more or less standard, and a simpler technology. It is a "coarse structure" theory, the contribution of which is to show that the demand for goods shows broad substitution properties. It is not a "fine structure" theory, designed to handle the effects of product variation on demand and other problems involving relatively small differences in the characteristics associated with different goods. The "goods" of traditional theory are typically such aggregates as "automobiles," "food," "clothing," rather than individual goods as strictly defined.

The concept of "characteristics" or "attributes" is not new in itself and, as already pointed out, was inherent in the work of Menger,[10] with some traces also in Chamberlin.[11] An explicit development of the consumption technology approach was used in the formulation of the diet problem by Cornfield[12] and its later study by Stigler.[13]

In the 1950s references to the idea can be seen in the writing of Brems,[14] Theil,[15] and Houthakker.[16] More explicit use of characteristics was made by May,[17] whose primary interest was in the effect on the transitivity properties of preference functions expressed in terms of goods rather than characteristics. Hicks[18] reached the point of stating the fundamentals of the analysis quite explicitly, in a Mengerian way: "It would accordingly appear that we ought to think of the consumer as choosing, according to his preferences, between certain *objectives;* and then deciding, more or less as the entrepreneur decides, between alternative *means* of reaching those objectives. The commodities which he purchases are for the most part means to the attainment of objectives, not objectives themselves." Unfortunately, after a brief examination of the possibilities, Hicks concluded that the technical difficulties of the approach made it not worth development.

None of these approaches mentioned attempted, however, to integrate the characteristics approach into the central core of demand

---

[10] *Ibid.*

[11] E. H. Chamberlin, *The Theory of Monopolistic Competition*, Harvard, 1933.

[12] Jerome Cornfield, unpublished memorandum, 1941.

[13] G. J. Stigler, "An Analysis of the diet problem," *Journal of Farm Economics*, May, 1945.

[14] Hans Brems, *Product Equilibrium under Monopolistic Competition*, Harvard, 1951.

[15] H. H. Theil, "Qualities, prices and budget enquiries," *Review of Economic Studies*, Vol. 19, No. 2, 1952.

[16] H. S. Houthakker, "Compensated changes in quantities and qualities consumed," *Review of Economic Studies*, Vol. 19, No. 3, 1952.

[17] K. O. May, "Intransitivity, utility and the aggregation of preference patterns," *Econometrica*, Vol. 22, January, 1954.

[18] J. R. Hicks, *A Revision of Demand Theory*, Oxford, 1956, p. 166.

theory. The work on the diet problem, in which the basic elements for a complete analysis are present, concentrated only on subsistence and failed to take account of the divergence of preferences between individuals. With the war over, this specific approach was too narrow and the analytics of the problem were digested into the more technical developments associated with the growth of linear programming and activity analysis.

In recent years the limitations of a simple approach that implies an immediate transformation of goods into "utility" or whatever the consumer is supposed to derive from his consumption, has been recognized. Becker[19] and others have developed the idea of consumption as a process, that may involve inputs (the comsumer's time, for example) additional to the goods themselves. That the characteristics of goods, rather than the goods per se, are what really count has been implicit in attempts to develop "hedonic" price indexes that represent constant-characteristics[20,21] rather than constant-goods collections. When faced with such problems as estimating the demand for forms of transport which may not yet exist, the economist is forced into a characteristics approach, whereby estimates are attempted of the demand for various characteristics of travel, the demand for a hypothetical mode of travel being synthesized from these.[22]

The aim of the present work is to provide a fully integrated theory of consumer choice and demand, in which the characteristics of goods are taken explicitly into account, as an alternative to ad hoc models devised to deal with special situations. Such a theory, as the reader will discover, provides a basic structure within which product variations and new goods fit easily and naturally. The demand for a new good could, in principle, be predicted from observed behavior with respect to existing goods, provided the new good possesses the same characteristics (although in a different combination) as those existing. Whether goods are close substitutes or not is shown to depend (as expected) on their characteristics, and, in principle, the closeness of substitution

[19] G. S. Becker, "A theory of the allocation of time," *Economic Journal*, September, 1965.

[20] Z. Griliches, "Hedonic price indexes for automobiles," in National Bureau of Economic Research, *Price Statistics of the Federal Government*, 1961.

[21] Z. Griliches and I. Adelman, "On an index of quality change," *Journal of the American Statistical Association*, 1961, pp. 535–48.

[22] R. E. Quandt and W. J. Baumol, "The demand for abstract transport modes: theory and measurement," *Journal of Regional Science*, Vol. 6, 1966, pp. 13–26.

could be predicted from technical data concerning characteristics. The characteristics model separates properties of demand which are universal and depend on characteristics from those which depend only on the special preferences of individuals, as contrasted with the traditional approach in which universal and technical properties are inseparably compounded with personal preferences.

The relationship between the theory of demand and consumer behavior set out here and the traditional theory is very simple: traditional theory is shown to be a special case of the more general theory. In other words, what is presented is a more general theory than the traditional one, not a theory which is at odds with, or contradictory to, the tradition.

1.5   Scope of This Study

Several volumes could be written on this subject, each exploring some aspect of the characteristics model: its applications to demand theory and to intertemporal choice, the welfare implications, a theory of product differentiation, and so on. The aim of this study is primarily to develop the implications of the simplest characteristics model (the linear model) for static demand theory and to lay the foundations for operational application in this area. Although other possible lines of development are touched on at various points, the emphasis is very definitely on static demand theory.[23]

The first part of the book is devoted to the basic development of the characteristics approach, largely in terms of a linear technology, and its application to demand theory. We shall find that there are efficiency effects common to all consumers as well as demand effects which depend on individual preferences, as all demand effects do in the traditional model. We shall also find that aggregate behavior cannot be expressed in terms of the traditional "representative consumer" because different groups of consumers will react only to different groups of goods and their price changes. Thus we shall be led to explore simple models of distributed preferences. We shall find that something can be said about substitutability between goods on the basis of objective technical data alone.

The second part of the book explores the requirements for making the

[23] For development of the characteristics approach into some other areas, see M. S. van Praag, *Individual Welfare Functions and Consumer Behavior*, North-Holland, 1968.

characteristics approach operationally useful. It is concerned with such matters as whether we can analyze groups of goods in relative isolation from other groups, just what constitutes an operational characteristic, criteria for determining whether a given characteristic can or cannot be omitted in analyzing a particular group, and other problems affecting operational employment of the theory.

The book is concerned primarily with consumer demand. Some reference is made to the possible extension of the analysis into the area of other consumer decisions, such as occupational choice. The analysis is readily, and perhaps more easily, applicable to demand of firms for inputs, including labor of various kinds and equipment, where the input's impact on the firm's operations cannot be expressed in a single dimension. For the firm the preference function can presumably be expressed more objectively and explicitly than for the consumer.

Part I

THE THEORY

CHAPTER 2

THE BASIC REFERENCE MODEL

2.1 The Consumption Technology

The simplest characteristics model, and the one that we shall use as our basic reference, to be added to, modified, and complicated as the analysis proceeds, is that based on the assumption of a linear additive relationship between goods and characteristics. We assume at the outset, in this model, that all characteristics are quantitative and objectively measurable so that the assertion that b_{ij} is the quantity of the ith characteristic possessed by a unit amount of the jth good has universal and (in principle) empirical meaning. The "unit" in which a particular characteristic is measured is unimportant except that it must be the same for all goods possessing the characteristic and maintained throughout the analysis.

If b_{ij} is the quantity of the ith characteristic possessed by a unit amount of the jth good, and z_i, x_j are quantities of the ith characteristic and jth good, respectively, the essential assumptions of the model are as follows.

Linearity. $z_i = b_{ij}x_j$, that is, quantity x_j of the jth good possesses x_j times as much of each characteristic as does unit quantity of that good.

Additivity. $z_i = b_{ij}x_j + b_{ik}x_k$, that is, given quantities of the two goods x_j and x_k, the total amount of the ith characteristic possessed by the goods collection (x_j, x_k) is the sum of the amounts of the characteristic possessed by x_j, x_k, separately.

It follows that, in a system of r characteristics and n goods, the collection of characteristics possessed by some collection $(x_1, \ldots, x_n)$ of the n goods is given by

$$z_i = \sum_{j=1}^{n} b_{ij} x_j \qquad i = 1, \ldots, r$$

In matrix terms, to which we shall adhere for the remainder of the analysis:

$$z = Bx$$

where $z = [z_i]$ is the vector of characteristics, $x = [x_j]$ the vector of goods, and $B = [b_{ij}]$ the matrix of coefficients relating goods and characteristics or *consumption technology matrix*.

Note that the relationship $z = Bx$ implies a unique characteristics vector (z) associated with a given goods vector (x). It does not imply a unique goods vector associated with a specified characteristics vector or, for that matter, that an arbitrary characteristics vector can be attained from a feasible goods collection at all. This point will be discussed later in the analysis, but note should be taken of it here at the beginning.

Since the consumption technology matrix B is so central to the analysis, its nature and properties should be made clear from the outset.

First, it should be stressed that no relationship between the number of goods (n) and the number of characteristics (r) has yet been suggested. We might have $r > n$, $r < n$, or $r = n$. Thus the matrix B is a general rectangular matrix and not, except in the case of the special coincidence $r = n$, a square matrix. Although, in a general sense, the elements b_{ij} of B are "input-output" coefficients in that they represent a fixed ratio between the input of a good and the output of a characteristic, the analog with input-output analysis in production theory cannot be pursued far. Whereas in production input-output models (particularly the Leontief versions) the set of outputs coincides completely (in the closed Leontief model) or almost so (in the open model) with the set of inputs, here the set of "outputs" is a set of characteristics and the set of "inputs" is a set of goods. Thus the fundamental relationship $z = Bx$ in our model represents a linear transformation from one space (goods or G-space) into another (characteristics or C-space), rather than a transformation from goods space into goods space, as in input-output. In later elaborations we shall examine cases in which some characteristics appear as inputs as well as outputs, but the central core of the analysis is concerned with relations between a set of goods and a set of characteristics quite distinct from them.

Because B is the matrix of a transformation from one space into another, there is no relationship (as in input-output) between the units in which characteristics are measured and those in which goods are measured. If, for example, we halve the size of the units in which the ith characteristic is measured, we need to double the coefficients b_{ij} for all j (that is, the ith row in B), but that is all. In an input-output model we need to double the coefficients in the kth row *and* in the kth column.

Table 2.1   A Diet Example

Characteristic	Milk ($\frac{1}{2}$ pt.)	Eggs (1)	Sirloin Steak (3 oz.)	Oranges (1)	Bread (1 loaf)
Calories (no.)	160	80	330	60	1225
Protein (mg.)	9	6	20	2	39
Vitamin A (international units)	350	590	50	240	...

Looked at as composed of rows or columns, the matrix B can be visualized as follows:

In terms of its columns B^j: Since B^j is the column vector $[b_{ij}]$, $i = 1, \ldots, r$, it represents the collection of characteristics possessed by unit quantity of the jth good.

In terms of its rows B_i: Since B_i is the row vector, $[b_{ij}], j = 1, \ldots, n$, it is best visualized as an array showing the relative amounts of ith characteristic possessed by unit quantities of each of the n goods. It has little significance of itself, since each entry depends on the unit in which that good is measured.

We can use a real example which illustrates the structure of the linear additive model. Suppose the only goods in the system are foods, and the only characteristics are nutrients. The b_{ij}'s, giving amounts of each nutrient (a vitamin, calories, protein, or a mineral) per unit quantity of each food, are objective and measurable, and have been measured and tabulated by official agencies for most foods. Furthermore, the food-nutrient relationship is linear and additive. Thus we can, in fact, construct a consumption technology matrix for this system, as in Table 2.1, drawn up for 3 nutrients and 5 foods.

Given some specified goods collection, say 1 pint of milk, 3 oranges, and 1 loaf of bread, the characteristics collection (1725 calories, 63 mg. protein, 1420 units vitamin A) is unique. But the same characteristics collection can be derived from other goods collections, for example, from approximately $1\frac{3}{4}$ pints of milk, 2 oranges, and $1\frac{1}{4}$ loaves of bread (exact figures: 1.735, 2.05, 1.245).

In this table, b_{23}, for example, is the amount of protein per unit of steak. B^3, the third column, gives the collection of the nutrients in one unit of steak, while B_2, the second row, gives the amounts of protein in unit quantities of the 5 foods.

At this stage we consider that, in principle, the B matrix represents the whole consumption technology, so that it covers all goods and all characteristics relevant to the society (or sub-society) under consideration. Later we shall investigate structural and context properties that enable us to concentrate on a part, only, of the whole matrix.

We shall initially assume, again subject to later modification, that all characteristics are measured as essentially non-negative quantities and that goods are also essentially non-negative. Thus the elements b_{ij} are non-negative and B is a non-negative matrix. We can make the somewhat stronger assumption that B is a semipositive matrix, having at least one positive entry in every row and every column. This ensures that our tabulation of the technology does not include any good which has none of the relevant characteristics or any characteristic which is not possessed by at least one of the goods.

From the relationship $z = Bx$, semipositivity of B implies that $z \geqq 0$ if $x \geqq 0$ and $z \geq 0$ if $x \geq 0$. The latter implication is that there is a positive quantity of at least one characteristic if there is a positive amount of at least one good.

Finally, the assumption of universality and objectivity should be stressed. Every person in the economy is assumed to "see" the same consumption technology just as, in basic production theory, every producer sees the same production technology. Whatever differences exist between persons as to how they view a given collection of characteristics with respect to themselves, it is assumed there is no difference between them as to what collection of characteristics is associated with any specified collection of goods.

Operationally speaking, it is universality that is important. If everyone believes that snake oil has special medical properties, we would analyze behavior as though this were indeed true even if, in some objective sense, it could not be shown to be true; or even if it could be shown to be false, provided the negative proof was unknown or un-accepted in the society being studied.

2.2   The Traditional Analysis as a Special Case

The traditional analysis of consumer behavior can be regarded as the analysis of a linear additive model having the following special structure for the B matrix: (i) the number of goods equals the number of characteristics ($r = n$), so that B is square; (ii) each row contains one and only one non-zero element, and each column contains one and only one non-zero element.

A matrix with this structure can be permuted, by a suitable ordering of the characteristics, so that all the non-zero elements lie down the leading diagonal. Thus we can write B as a diagonal matrix where $b_{ii} > 0$, all i; $b_{ij} = 0$ for $i \neq j$.

The goods-characteristics relationship is now of the form

$$z_i = b_{ii}x_i \qquad i = 1, \ldots, n$$

This is simply equivalent to associating a single characteristic with each good ("butterness" with butter), which can be derived from no other good. The characteristics differ from goods only in name and in units of measurement, with respect to which the analysis of consumer behavior is invariant. Thus we obtain the traditional analysis in which we can deal directly with goods rather than with characteristics.

In this traditional case, since B is square and has non-zero elements down its leading diagonal which render it non-singular, the inverse transformation

$$x = B^{-1}z$$

exists. Thus the relationship between x and z is one-to-one in both directions, giving the traditional model.

Note that the case in which B is square (number of goods equal to number of characteristics), but cannot be permuted into a diagonal matrix, will also give an inverse transformation $z = B^{-1}x$ (unless B is singular), but is not equivalent to the traditional model. We shall show later that a technology of this kind leads to demand properties, such as dominance of the market by a single good at certain prices, that are not possessed by the traditional model.

2.3   Preferences

The consumption technology expresses the relationship between characteristics and goods. The relationship between characteristics and people is expressed by their preferences. We assume that the interest of consumers is in characteristics, not in goods per se. Thus the individual consumer has preferences, in the first instance, over the set of characteristics collections. Any preferences concerning collections of goods are derived preferences, a particular goods collection being preferred over another only because the collection of characteristics associated with the former is preferred to the collection of characteristics associated with the latter.

At this stage we do not wish to investigate the structure of preferences but will simply carry over traditional preference theory, applying it to collections of characteristics instead of to collections of goods. The assumptions of traditional preference theory, modified for our use, are:

(1) The consumer has a complete quasi-ordering over the set of all possible characteristics collections. Using the symbols P ("preferred to"), $\bar{P}$ ("not preferred to"), I ("indifferent between"), this requires, in particular, that:

(a) If $z^1 P z^2$ and $z^2 P z^3$, then $z^1 P z^3$ (transitivity), with equivalents for the relationships $\bar{P}$ and I.

(b) For every pair of vectors z^1, z^2, either $z^1 \bar{P} z^2$ or $z^2 \bar{P} z^1$ (completeness).

(2) For any characteristics collection z^*, the upper and lower preference sets, $\{z \mid z^* \bar{P} z\}$ and $\{z \mid z \bar{P} z^*\}$ are closed (continuity)

(3) For any two collections z^1, z^2 such that $z^1 I z^2$, any strong convex combination of z^1 and z^2 (i.e., $z^* = \lambda z^1 + (1 - \lambda)z^2$, $0 < \lambda < 1$) is preferred to either z^1 or z^2 (strict convexity).

Assumptions (1), (2), and (3) are sufficient to guarantee that there exists some continuous function $u(z)$ such that $u(z^1) > u(z^2)$ if and only if $z^1 P z^2$, and $u(z^1) = u(z^2)$ if and only if $z^1 I z^2$ and, furthermore, that this function is strictly concave-contoured (strictly quasi-concave). In other words, these three assumptions enable us to summarize the consumer's preferences in terms of a utility function whose contours (indifference curves) are strictly convex toward the origin.

Two other assumptions that are explicit or implicit in most traditional preference theory will also be made provisionally, although these will be subject to later reexamination:

(4) For any collection z^*, there is some collection z such that zPz^* (*non-satiation*).

(5) For any two collections z^1, z^2 such that $z^1 - z^2 \geqslant 0$ (z^1 has more of at least one characteristic, and no less of any other, than z^2), we have z^1Pz^2 (*all characteristics positively desired*).

The last two assumptions, together with the first three, guarantee that the consumer's preferences can be expressed in terms of an ordinal utility function of the neoclassical kind with all its first-order partial derivatives positive.

Finally, we make the essential behavioral assumption without which our preference structure would be useless:

The consumer acts in accordance with his preferences, that is, given the opportunity to choose from some set Z of characteristics collections, the consumer will choose that collection which maximizes u(z) over Z.

2.4 Choice with a Budget Constraint

The consumer is assumed to act in accordance with his preferences, and thus his behavior in a given choice situation will be as though he were maximizing a utility index over the feasible set of available choices.

What distinguishes, at the outset, the choice situation in the characteristics model from that in the traditional model of the consumer is that the objective function $u(z)$ of the optimizing problem in the characteristics approach is a function of characteristics, while the regular budget constraint is a constraint on goods.

Let p be the vector of prices facing the consumer and k be his income in terms of money or the numeraire good. Then the regular budget constraint (fixed income and fixed prices independent of the consumer's actions) has the form

$$px \leqq k$$

The utility function has the form $u(z)$, while z, x are linked through the goods-characteristics relationship

$$z = Bx$$

Thus the consumer's choice problem under a regular budget constraint can be formulated as the optimizing problem:

$$\text{Max } u(z)$$
$$\text{S.T. } z = Bx$$
$$x \geqq 0$$
$$px \leqq k$$

(Under our provisional assumption that $B \geqq 0$, we do not need to add $z \geqq 0$ as a separate constraint. In later elaborations we may need to take account of this constraint separately.)

Since the objective function is defined in characteristics space (C-space) and the feasible set by constraints in goods space (G-space), a solution necessitates bringing the objective function and the feasible set into the same space by mapping one of them into the space of the other. The linking relationship is, of course, $z = Bx$.

We have the choice of expressing either the utility function in terms of goods or the constraints in terms of characteristics.

Since the consumption technology gives characteristics uniquely in terms of goods, the most obvious choice might seem to map the utility function into goods space. We can substitute $z = Bx$ in the utility function to obtain the consumer's optimizing problem in the form

$$\text{Max} \ \ u(Bx) = v(x)$$
$$\text{S.T.} \ \ px \leqq k, \qquad x \geqq 0$$

In this form, the problem has a deceptive resemblance to the simple traditional case. There are, however, major differences if the number of characteristics is less than the number of goods. Suppose there are r characteristics and n ($> r$) goods. Then the partial derivatives of v with respect to the goods (x_j) and the partial derivatives of u with respect to the characteristics (z_i) are related by

$$\frac{\partial v}{\partial x_j} = \sum_{i=1}^{r} b_{ij} \frac{\partial u}{\partial z_i} \qquad j = 1, \ldots, n$$

Since there are only r derivatives $\partial u / \partial z_i$, it follows that $n - r$ of the derivatives $\partial v / \partial x_j$ can be expressed in terms of the remaining r. Thus not all the first-order conditions of the traditional solution

$$\frac{\partial v}{\partial x_j} = \lambda_j p_j$$

can necessarily be satisfied. We cannot use the simple neoclassical optimizing technique but must use the more complex techniques of nonlinear programming.

In geometric terms the linear dependence between the partial derivatives of $v(x)$ means that the indifference surfaces of v in goods space are not strictly convex to the origin, even if the indifference surfaces of u in characteristics space are, but have "flats" in certain directions. Thus corner solutions become general, and the simplicity of the traditional case is lost.

A more important objection to transforming the utility function into goods space, and one that is decisive in the context of this book, is that *the universal and objective consumption technology is swallowed up into each individual's private and subjective utility function.*

The "swallowing up" does not mean simply that, in the absence of prior information about the detailed properties of $u(z)$, we could replace it by an arbitrary $v(x)$ with traditional properties and ignore the existence of the consumption technology. On the contrary, the function $v(x)$ has part of its properties (like the linear dependence among its partial derivatives) determined by the consumption technology, part by the individual properties of the particular $u(z)$ with which we started.

The properties from the technology (which apply to all consumers in a class) and those from the personal eccentricities of the individual, become extremely difficult to disentangle once the utility function has been mapped into goods space. We shall see, after the analysis of the next two chapters, that we can quite easily have situations in which:

(1) There are certain corner solutions which are universal in the sense that no consumers, whatever their personal utility functions $u(z)$, will consume certain of the goods.

(2) There are other corner solutions which are universal over all consumers whose utility functions belong to a particular class, with other corner solutions for consumers with other classes of utility functions. In other words, there are some groups of consumers that will not consume good i and other groups that will consume good i but not good j.

(3) Finally, there are variations among consumers in a group in the individual choices of quantities of the various goods.

When the utility functions are mapped into goods space some of these effects will be due to the existence of "flats" on the indifference surfaces of $v(x)$, some of the flats being common to all consumers, some to consumers only in one group, while other effects will depend on curvature of the surfaces (personal). The properties are as difficult to track down as to describe.

The inverse approach to the problem, mapping the budget set into characteristics space, has its own problems. Since, in general, the number of goods is not equal to the number of characteristics, the goods-characteristics relationship $z = Bx$ does not have a unique inverse giving x in terms of z and thus $px \leqq k$ as a constraint on z by simple substitution. However, there is one feature of the mapping which more than outweighs all its problems:

The one mapping will suffice for all consumers facing the same market conditions.

The universality of the mapping of the feasible set from goods space into characteristics space is a consequence of the following:

(1) For consumers facing the same market conditions, the individual budget constraints $px \leqq k$ differ only in the value of k, the income.

(2) The goods-characteristics relationship $z = Bx$ is the same for all consumers.

(3) This relationship is also linear, so that if x^* maps into z^*, λx^* maps into λz^*. This means that the feasible sets (in characteristics space) of different consumers are simply related by scalar expansion or contraction in proportion to the ratios of their incomes.

Before passing on to discuss the solution of the problem by mapping into characteristics space, it should be made clear that the optimization problem for a particular individual may be performed either way. Both methods are correct, but we have chosen the one that throws most light on the universal properties of choice and demand.

CHAPTER 3

ANALYSIS IN CHARACTERISTICS SPACE

3.1 The Feasible Set

In Chapter 2 we rejected, as unnecessarily disguising the universal properties of demand, the analysis of the consumer optimizing problem by mapping the individual utility functions into goods space. We now proceed to discuss the alternative—mapping the budget constraints into characteristics space.

The budget set in goods space is defined by the budget hyperplane $px = k$ and the non-negativity constraints on quantities of goods. If the technology matrix, B, is square and non-singular, the relationship $z = Bx$ has a unique inverse $x = B^{-1}z$ so that the budget hyperplane can be written immediately as $pB^{-1}z = k$ and is thus a hyperplane in characteristics space. In the general case, however, the budget hyperplane does not map into a hyperplane in characteristics space, and any simple geometric analogy between the traditional depiction of the budget set in goods space and its image in characteristics space no longer exists.

Formally, we have a budget set in G-space (goods space) defined as $\{x \mid px \leq k, x \geq 0\}$. The image of this in C-space (characteristics space) is the set $K = \{z \mid z = Bx, px \leq k, x \geq 0\}$. We are interested in the general properties of K and the dependence of these properties on the technology B, the price vector p, and the income k.

The budget set in G-space is a convex set and the mapping $z = Bx$

is linear, so that K will be a convex set in C-space. More specifically, the budget set in G-space is a convex polytope (polyhedral set) bounded by the coordinate hyperplanes and the budget hyperplane. It has exactly $n + 1$ extreme points[1]—the origin and the n points of intersection between the budget hyperplane and each of the coordinate axes. The point of intersection between the budget hyperplane and the sth coordinate axis has coordinates $x_s^s = k/p_s$, $x_j^s = 0$ for $j \neq s$.

It is a fundamental property of any convex set that it can be defined completely in terms of its extreme points and that, in particular, it is the set of all convex combinations[2] of its extreme points. Thus the budget set in G-space is the set of all convex combinations of the $n + 1$ points:

$$\begin{bmatrix} 0 \\ 0 \\ . \\ . \\ 0 \end{bmatrix} \begin{bmatrix} k/p_1 \\ 0 \\ . \\ . \\ 0 \end{bmatrix} \begin{bmatrix} 0 \\ k/p_2 \\ . \\ . \\ 0 \end{bmatrix} \cdots \begin{bmatrix} 0 \\ 0 \\ . \\ . \\ k/p_n \end{bmatrix}$$

Owing to the linearity of the mapping, any point that is a convex combination of two points in G-space with certain weights will have an image in C-space which is a convex combination of the images of those same two points, with the same weights. Thus the image set, K, of the budget set is the set of all convex combinations of the images of the extreme points of the budget set.

The image of the G-space origin is, of course, the C-space origin.

The remaining n extreme points in G-space are of the kind x^s, where $x_s^s = k/p_s$ and $x_j^s = 0$ for $j \neq s$. The image, z^s, of such a point is given by

$$z^s = Bx^s$$

with the coordinates given by

$$z_i^s = \sum_j b_{ij} x_j^s$$

$$= (k/p_s) b_{is}$$

[1] An extreme point of a convex set is, geometrically speaking, a point which does not lie on any line segment joining two other points of the set. An extreme point is necessarily a boundary point, but a boundary point need not be an extreme point. Extreme points will be either "corners" or points on curved sections of the boundary.

[2] A convex combination of vectors is a weighted sum of these vectors with nonnegative weights that add to unity. A strong convex combination exists if none of the weights is zero.

To simplify the notation, denote by q_j the reciprocal of the jth price $(1/p_j)$ so that we have

$$z_i^s = kq_s b_{is}$$

and the point z^s, the image of x^s, is the sth column B^s of the technology matrix multiplied by the scalar kq_s. That is,

$$z^s = kq_s B^s$$

Thus K is the set of all convex combinations of the $n + 1$ points $O, z^1, \ldots, z^s, \ldots, z^n$. These properties then follow immediately:

(1) K is a convex polytope, being the set of all convex combinations of a finite number of points.

(2) K has, at most, $n + 1$ extreme points, since a convex polytope defined on m points cannot have more than that number of extreme points.

(3) Every extreme point of K is the image of an extreme point in the budget set, since every point in the budget set which can be expressed as a strong convex combination of other points in the set (and is thus not an extreme point[3]) must have an image which is also a strong convex combination of points in the image set and thus is not an extreme point of K.[4]

(4) An extreme point of the budget set is not necessarily an extreme point of K, however. This property, which is extremely important in demand analysis, may not be immediately obvious.

To see how an extreme point of the budget set might fail to map into an extreme point of K, consider a technology with the number of goods (n) greater than the number of characteristics (r). Let x^* be an extreme point of the budget set whose image in K is z^*, given by $z^* = Bx^*$.

Now concentrate on the inverse problem: given z^*, to find a point x which maps into z^*. Such a point must satisfy the equation system

$$Bx = z^*$$

Since this is a system of r equations in $n(> r)$ unknowns $x_1, \ldots, x_n$, it will typically have multiple solutions. In particular, we can find up to

[3] The geometric definition of an extreme point, given in footnote 1, is equivalent to the statement that an extreme point cannot be written as the strong convex combination of points in the set.

[4] We can state the property in an alternative way. The image of any non-extreme point of the budget set cannot be an extreme point of K, since the image can be expressed as the same strong convex combination of other image points as the original could be of points in the budget set.

$\binom{n-r}{r}$ basic solutions by putting any $n - r$ of the unknowns equal to zero and solving for the remaining r as an ordinary square system.

Not all these basic solutions will necessarily satisfy the budget constraint $px \leqq k$ or the nonnegativity constraints $x \geqq 0$. At least one basic feasible solution (x^*) exists, however, by definition of z^* as the image of x^*.

Should there be a second basic solution x^{**} which is also feasible then, from linear equation theory, the combination $x = \lambda x^* + (1 - \lambda)x^{**}$ $(0 < \lambda < 1)$ is also a feasible solution. Thus z^* must be the image of x as well as of x^*. But x is a strong convex combination of two points (x^*, x^{**}) in the budget set and cannot be an extreme point of K, since it is the image of a non-extreme point of the budget set, as well as of an extreme point.

z^* will be an extreme point of K if and only if the system $Bx = z^*$, $px \leqq k$, $x \geqq 0$ has a *unique* basic feasible solution x^* which is an extreme point of the budget set.

3.2   Numerical Examples

The general properties of the mapping from the budget set in G-space to the feasible set in C-space can readily be illustrated by simple numerical examples and associated diagrams. Five examples are given here.

Example 1
We have

$$B = \begin{bmatrix} 2 & 1.8 & 1 \\ 1 & 1.8 & 2 \end{bmatrix} \qquad p = [1, 1, 1] \qquad k = 1$$

The budget set in G-space is the tetrahedron bounded by the co-ordinate planes and the budget plane $x_1 + x_2 + x_3 = 1$. Its extreme points are

$$0 = \begin{bmatrix} 0 \\ 0 \\ 0 \end{bmatrix}; \qquad x^1 = \begin{bmatrix} 1 \\ 0 \\ 0 \end{bmatrix}; \qquad x^2 = \begin{bmatrix} 0 \\ 1 \\ 0 \end{bmatrix}; \qquad x^3 = \begin{bmatrix} 0 \\ 0 \\ 1 \end{bmatrix}$$

The set is illustrated in Figure 3.1(a).

The transformation between G-space and C-space is determined by the relationships

$$z_1 = 2x_1 + 1.8x_2 + x_3$$
$$z_2 = x_1 + 1.8x_2 + 2x_3$$

so that the images of 0, x^1, x^2, x^3 in C-space are, respectively:

$$0 = \begin{bmatrix} 0 \\ 0 \end{bmatrix} ; \quad z^1 = \begin{bmatrix} 2 \\ 1 \end{bmatrix} ; \quad z^2 = \begin{bmatrix} 1.8 \\ 1.8 \end{bmatrix} ; \quad z^3 = \begin{bmatrix} 1 \\ 2 \end{bmatrix}$$

K is the set of all convex combinations of 0, z^1, z^2, z^3 and is represented by the kite-shaped area in Figure 3.1(b). In this case, every extreme point of the budget set maps into an extreme point of k.

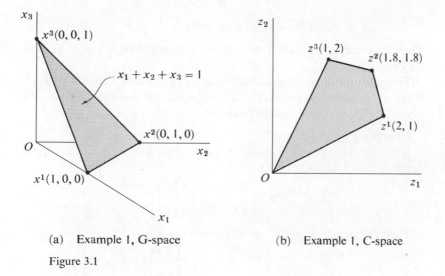

(a)   Example 1, G-space   (b)   Example 1, C-space

Figure 3.1

z^2, in this example, is an extreme point of K because it is the image of x^2, an extreme point of the budget set, and because no other point in the budget set maps into z^2.

Since z^2 has coordinates $[1.8, 1.8]$, any point which maps into it must have coordinates satisfying the equations

$$2x_1 + 1.8x_2 + x_3 = 1.8$$
$$x_1 + 1.8x_2 + 2x_3 = 1.8$$

It is easily seen that this system has only two basic solutions

$$x^* = \begin{bmatrix} 0 \\ 1 \\ 0 \end{bmatrix}; \qquad x^{**} = \begin{bmatrix} 0.6 \\ 0 \\ 0.6 \end{bmatrix}$$

If x is a possible solution, it must be expressible in the form

$$x = \lambda x^* + (1 - \lambda)x^{**} = \begin{bmatrix} 0.6(1 - \lambda) \\ \lambda \\ 0.6(1 - \lambda) \end{bmatrix}$$

To satisfy the budget constraint, we must have

$$x_1 + x_2 + x_3 = 1$$

that is,

$$0.6(1 - \lambda) + \lambda + 0.6(1 - \lambda) \leq 1$$

Thus we must have $\lambda \geq 1$. But x is not non-negative if $\lambda > 1$, so that we must have $\lambda = 1$.

Thus z^2 is the image of the single point x^*, which is identical with x^2. Since x^2 is an extreme point of the budget set and the only point which maps into z^2, z^2 is an extreme point of K.

Example 2

Now consider the same budget constraint, but with the mapping determined by the technology

$$B = \begin{bmatrix} 2 & 1.2 & 1 \\ 1 & 1.2 & 2 \end{bmatrix}$$

Then the points O, x^1, x^2, x^3 map into

$$O = \begin{bmatrix} 0 \\ 0 \end{bmatrix}; \qquad z^1 = \begin{bmatrix} 2 \\ 1 \end{bmatrix}; \qquad z^2 = \begin{bmatrix} 1.2 \\ 1.2 \end{bmatrix}; \qquad z^3 = \begin{bmatrix} 1 \\ 2 \end{bmatrix}$$

and K is the triangular area in Figure 3.2. Here z^2, the image of x^2, is an interior point of the triangle and thus clearly not an extreme point.

In algebraic terms, the point z^2 ($= [1.2, 1.2]$) can be expressed as a strong convex combination of the extreme points O, z^1, z^3 in the following form:

$$z^2 = 1.2[O] + 0.4z^1 + 0.4z^3$$

which gives the more formal proof that it is not an extreme point.

Note that x^2 is not the only point in the budget set having the image [1.2, 1.2] in C-space. All points ζ giving this image will have co-ordinates satisfying the equations

$$2\zeta_1 + 1.2\zeta_2 + \zeta_3 = 1.2$$
$$\zeta_1 + 1.2\zeta_2 + \zeta_3 = 1.2$$

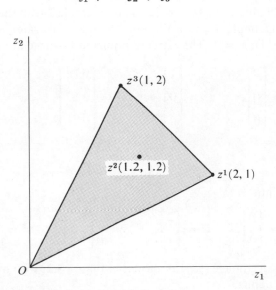

Figure 3.2. Examples 2 and 3, C-space

and the budget inequalities $\zeta_1, \zeta_2, \zeta_3 \geqq 0$

$$\zeta_1 + \zeta_2 + \zeta_3 \geqq 1$$

It is easy to show that the only basic feasible solutions (that is having at least one zero coordinate) are

$$\zeta^* = \begin{bmatrix} 0 \\ 1 \\ 0 \end{bmatrix} = x^2 \quad \text{and} \quad \zeta^{**} = \begin{bmatrix} 0.4 \\ 0 \\ 0.4 \end{bmatrix} = 0.4x^1 + 0.4x^3$$

The latter can be written as $0.2[O] + 0.4x^1 + 0.4x^3$. It is the same convex combination of O, x^1, x^3 that z^2 was shown to be of O, z^1, z^3.

The complete set of points in G-space which map into [1.2, 1.2] in

C-space is the set

$$\{x \mid x = 0.4\lambda x^1 + (1 - \lambda)x^2 + 0.4\lambda x^3, \quad 0 \leq \lambda \leq 1\}$$

which is, in geometric terms, the line segment joining ζ^* and ζ^{**}.

Example 3
We would obtain the same effect as in Example 2 with the technology matrix of Example 1 and a different budget constraint, for instance $p = (1, 1.5, 1)$, $k = 1$. The extreme points in G-space are now

$$O = \begin{bmatrix} 0 \\ 0 \\ 0 \end{bmatrix}, \quad x^1 = \begin{bmatrix} 1 \\ 0 \\ 0 \end{bmatrix}, \quad x^2 = \begin{bmatrix} 0 \\ 0.67 \\ 0 \end{bmatrix}, \quad x^3 = \begin{bmatrix} 0 \\ 0 \\ 1 \end{bmatrix}$$

with

$$B = \begin{bmatrix} 2 & 1.8 & 1 \\ 1 & 1.8 & 2 \end{bmatrix}$$

these map into

$$O = \begin{bmatrix} 0 \\ 0 \end{bmatrix}, \quad z^1 = \begin{bmatrix} 2 \\ 1 \end{bmatrix}, \quad z^2 = \begin{bmatrix} 1.2 \\ 1.2 \end{bmatrix}, \quad z^3 = \begin{bmatrix} 1 \\ 2 \end{bmatrix}$$

giving the same image set K as shown in Figure 3.2, with only O, z^1, z^3 as extreme points.

All three examples serve to illustrate another property of the feasible set in C-space. Although points with $x_1 = 0$, $x_2 = 0$, and so on are all feasible in the budget set, points with $z_1 = 0$, $z_2 = 0$ do not necessarily exist in K (except for the origin itself). It is a matter of the technology whether goods exist which possess none of a given characteristic.

Example 4
Consider a case in which the number of characteristics is greater than the number of goods. This is illustrated by the technology

$$B = \begin{bmatrix} 2 & 1 \\ 1 & 1 \\ 1 & 2 \end{bmatrix}$$

and the budget constraint defined by $p = (1, 1)$, $k = 1$.

The extreme points of the budget set,

$$O = \begin{bmatrix} 0 \\ 0 \end{bmatrix}, \qquad x^1 = \begin{bmatrix} 1 \\ 0 \end{bmatrix}, \qquad x^2 = \begin{bmatrix} 0 \\ 1 \end{bmatrix}$$

The budget set and the image set in C-space are illustrated in Figures 3.3(a) and Figure 3.3(b). Although C-space is three-dimensional, K is a two-dimensional triangle.

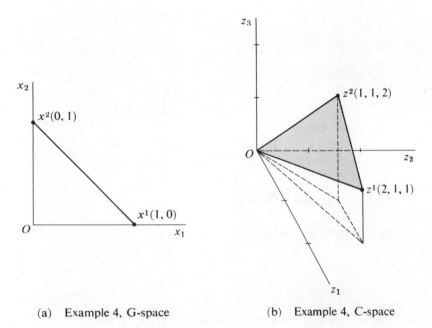

(a)   Example 4, G-space   (b)   Example 4, C-space

Figure 3.3

K lies entirely in the plane which passes through O, z^1, z^2. This has the equation

$$z_1 - 3z_2 + z_3 = 0$$

Example 5

This has been chosen to illustrate the point that equality between the number of goods and number of characteristics is necessary, but not sufficient, to give the traditional case in which K is defined by a budget hyperplane and coordinate planes just as in G-space.

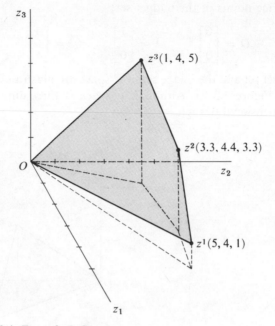

Figure 3.4. Example 5, C-space

Consider the 3 × 3 technology

$$B = \begin{bmatrix} 5 & 3.3 & 1 \\ 4 & 4.4 & 4 \\ 1 & 3.3 & 5 \end{bmatrix}$$

with the budget constraints defined by $p = [1, 1, 1]$, $k = 1$.
The extreme points of the budget set,

$$\begin{bmatrix} 0 \\ 0 \\ 0 \end{bmatrix}, \quad \begin{bmatrix} 1 \\ 0 \\ 0 \end{bmatrix}, \quad \begin{bmatrix} 0 \\ 1 \\ 0 \end{bmatrix}, \quad \begin{bmatrix} 0 \\ 0 \\ 1 \end{bmatrix}$$

map into

$$O = \begin{bmatrix} 0 \\ 0 \\ 0 \end{bmatrix}; \quad z^1 = \begin{bmatrix} 5 \\ 4 \\ 1 \end{bmatrix}; \quad z^2 = \begin{bmatrix} 4.4 \\ 4.4 \\ 3.3 \end{bmatrix}; \quad z^3 = \begin{bmatrix} 1 \\ 4 \\ 5 \end{bmatrix}$$

In this case, there is obvious linear dependence in the technology and B is singular. All points in the feasible set map into the plane $3z_1 - 2z_2 + 3z_3 = 0$. Within this plane, z^1, z^2, z^3 are all extreme points, and K is a kite-shaped planar set floating in three-dimensional C-space, as shown in Figure 3.4.

If B were non-singular, the feasible set in characteristics space would be a tetrahedron as in the traditional case, but the facet of the tetrahedron corresponding to the budget plane would not necessarily terminate on the coordinate axes. Termination on the coordinate axes would require that each good possessed only a single characteristic.

3.3 Efficient Choice

Having established the nature of the feasible set in C-space, that is, of the image in C-space of the budget set in G-space, we can proceed to examine the actual choice.

If K is the feasible set in C-space, the consumer's problem is:

$$\text{Max } u(z)$$

$$\text{S.T. } z \in K$$

Since the first partial derivatives of $u(z)$ are everywhere positive, given all five basic assumptions stated earlier, $u(z)$ has no critical points. It follows from basic optimizing theory that the optimum point is necessarily a *boundary point* of K, interior solutions being ruled out. Not all boundary points are potential optima, however. From assumption (5) of Chapter 2 (all characteristics positively desired), no point z such that $z \leq z'$ for some $z' \in K$ can be an optimum point. Thus all potential optimum points lie on the *outer* boundary of K. That is, any optimum point is a member of the set E such that

If $z \in E$, there is no other point $z' \in K$ such that $z' \geq z$.

Following the terminology of production theory, we shall refer to the set E as the *efficiency set* or *efficiency frontier* of K. Figures 3.5(a), (b), (c) show, in heavy lines, those parts of the feasible sets of Figures 3.1(b), 3.2, 3.3(b), respectively, which form the efficiency frontier.

We now establish the following:

(1) *Every point on the efficiency frontier in C-space is the image of a point on the budget hyperplane in G-space.*

(2) *A point on the budget hyperplane in G-space does not necessarily have its image on the efficiency frontier in C-space.*

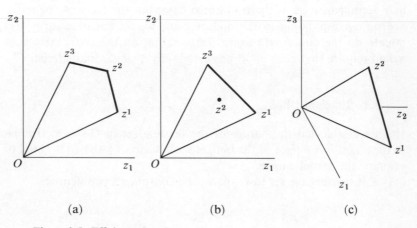

(a)   (b)   (c)

Figure 3.5. Efficiency frontiers

The first proposition comes from noting that, for any point x in the budget set which is not on the budget hyperplane, $px < k$, and thus there is some point x^* on the budget hyperplane such that $x^* \gg x$.

Since we have provisionally assumed that $B \geqslant 0$, it follows that

$$z^* - z' = B(x^* - x) \gg 0$$

so that z cannot lie on the efficiency frontier.

The second proposition has already been sufficiently established by showing that a point on the budget hyperplane in G-space may map into an interior point of the feasible set in C-space.

3.4 The Goods Efficiency Set

The goods efficiency set is the set of all attainable goods collections whose images lie on the efficiency frontier in C-space. Formally, the set is defined as

$$E_G = \{x \mid Bx \in E, px \leqq k, x \geqq 0\}$$

Let z^* be some point in E, and consider the set $S(z^*)$ of all goods collection having z^* as image in C-space. This is defined as

$$S(z^*) = \{x \mid Bx = z^*\}$$

$S(z^*)$ must contain at least one point, by definition of E.

Suppose we had $px < k$ for some $x \in S(z^*)$. Then $p(\lambda x) = k$ for some $\lambda > 1$, and x lies in the budget set. But if x has image z^* in C-space, λx must have image λz^* and $\lambda z^* \in E$. Since $z^* \ll \lambda z^*$, $z^* \notin E$, contrary to our original assertion. Thus we conclude that

$$px \geq k \quad \text{for all} \quad x \in S(z^*), \quad \text{where} \quad z^* \in E$$

Any point x^* in E_G which has image $z^* \in E$ must satisfy the budget constraint as well as be a member of $S(z^*)$, so that $px^* \leq k$ (budget constraint) and $px^* \geq k$ (membership of $S(z^*)$). Then we have $px^* = k$.

Since $px \geq k$ for all $x \in S(z^*)$, any $x^* \in S(z^*)$ which is also in the goods efficiency set must therefore minimize px over the set $S(z^*)$. In other words:

Every $x^* \in E_G$ is the solution of a canonical linear program:

$$Min\ px$$
$$S.T.\ Bx = z^*, x \geq 0$$

for some $z^* \in E$

This programming criterion is the chief analytical method for locating efficient goods collections, given optimal characteristics collections.

3.5 Classification of Optima

Let us now turn to the choice of the optimum characteristics collection. This has been reduced to the problem

$$Max\ u(z)$$
$$S.T.\ z \in K$$

where K is the image of the budget set in C-space. We know that if z^* is optimal, we shall have $z^* \in E$, where E is the efficiency frontier.

The set K has been shown to be a convex polytope, with each part of the outer boundary E a portion of a hyperplane, or of the intersection of hyperplanes. Every point in E is necessarily an extreme point, or a strong convex combination of extreme points, with O excluded.

Taking a geometrical view, rather than an algebraic one, we shall refer to points in E which are extreme points as *vertices*. A subset of E which consists entirely of convex combinations of some given set of $k(< r)$ extreme points, but cannot be expressed as a strong convex combination of more than k extreme points, will be referred to as an *edge of order k*. A subset of E consisting of points which can be expressed as strong convex combinations of r extreme points will be referred to as a *facet*.

If $r = 3$, the ideas above correspond to those of solid geometry, a facet having the dimensions of a plane, two facets intersecting in an edge with the dimension of a line (only edges of order 2 exist in 3-space), three facets typically intersecting in a vertex, which is also the intersection of the three edges formed by the pairwise intersection of the facets.

If $r = 2$, a facet is a line and a vertex a point. In Figure 3.5(a) for example, the vertices are z^1, z^2, z^3, with the facets z^1z^2 and z^2z^3. In Figure 3.5(b) there is a single facet and two vertices.

Figure 3.5(c) shows a single edge and two vertices, since $r = 3$.

For a regular utility function of the kind assumed, an optimal point $z^* \in E$ will lie on the highest contour (indifference surface) which is attainable. It is obvious that one of the following must be true:

(1) z^* lies in the interior of a facet, in which case the indifference surface $u(z) = u(z^*)$ must be tangent to the facet in every direction.

(2) z^* lies in the interior of an edge of order k, in which case the indifference surface $u(z) = u(z^*)$ must be tangent to the edge in the k dimensions of the edge.

(3) z^* lies on a vertex, in which case no tangency equations need to be met.

Proof of these propositions is trivial, along the standard lines of elementary economics.

Figure 3.6 illustrates possibilities (1) and (3) for an efficiency frontier of the kind shown in Figure 3.5(a). Points A, A' show possible optimal points on each of the two facets; B, B' possible vertex optima. Figure 3.7 illustrates possibility (2), with an edge optimum for the efficiency frontier of Figure 3.5(c). We shall now analyze these three types of optima in more detail.

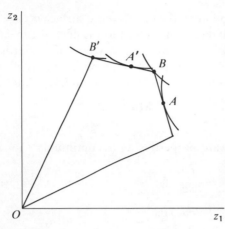

Figure 3.6. Facet and vertex optima

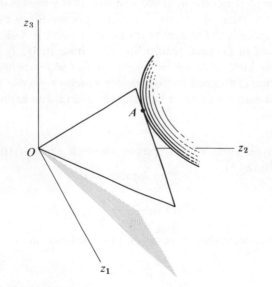

Figure 3.7. Edge optimum

3.6   Facet Optima

If z^* is a facet optimum, the indifference surface $u(z) = u(z^*)$ is tangent to the facet in all directions. The facet is part of some hyperplane with equation $wz = c = wz^*$. Since the vector w is normal to the facet, and every efficient facet has a strictly positive normal, we have $w \gg 0$.

Obviously, in this case z^* is the solution of an equivalent optimizing problem:

$$\text{Max } u(z)$$

$$\text{S.T. } wz \leqq c$$

with straightforward properties at the optimum:

$$\frac{\partial u}{\partial z_i} = \lambda w_i \qquad i = 1, \dots, r$$

or

$$\frac{\partial u}{\partial z_i} \bigg/ \frac{\partial u}{\partial z_j} = w_i/w_j \qquad \text{all } i, j$$

The w_i's will obviously turn out to be shadow prices of characteristics.

To further interpret the w_i's, we first note that a facet is defined as the convex combination of exactly r extreme points. Since every extreme point in C-space is the image of an extreme point in G-space, and an extreme point in G-space (excluding O, whose image is not in E) is a point of the kind $x_j^s = kg_j = kq_j$; $x_i^s = 0$, $i \neq j$ (where $q_j = 1/p_j$), a facet optimum is attained by consuming exactly r goods.

Thus each extreme point of the facet is given by an expression of the kind:

$$z^s = kq_j B^j$$

Since the hyperplane $wz = c$ passes through each of the r extreme points, we have

$$wz^s = kq_j w B^j = c$$

giving

$$wB^j = \frac{c}{kq_j} = \frac{c}{k} p_j$$

Over all r extreme points, this gives an equation system

$$w\hat{B} = \frac{c}{k} \hat{p}$$

where $\hat{B}$ is a square submatrix of B consisting of those r columns which correspond to the goods actually consumed and $\hat{p}$ is a truncated price vector consisting of the prices of the r goods actually consumed.

Since B is non-singular [otherwise not all the points in that particular set of extreme points in G-space could have extreme point images in C-space], we can solve uniquely for w to obtain

$$w = \frac{c}{k}\, \hat{p} \hat{B}^{-1}$$

This gives the equation of the facet in terms of the prices of the relevant set of goods and the consumption technology. Note that each

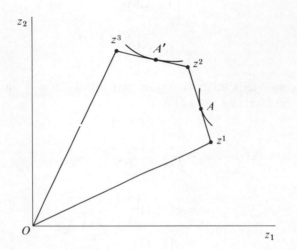

Figure 3.8. Facet optima

characteristic shadow price depends (in principle) on the prices of all goods relevant to that facet but is independent of the prices of goods not relevant to the facet, provided the facet in question remains efficient.

Example 1

Take the same 2×3 technology and budget constraint as in Example 1 in Chapter 3:

$$B = \begin{bmatrix} 2 & 1.8 & 1 \\ 1 & 1.8 & 2 \end{bmatrix}$$

$$p = [1, 1, 1] \qquad k = 1$$

Suppose the consumer's utility function is such as to give a point like A in Figure 3.8, on the facet $z^1 z^2$. The extreme points z^1, z^2 are the images of

$$x^1 = \begin{bmatrix} 1 \\ 0 \\ 0 \end{bmatrix}; \qquad x^2 = \begin{bmatrix} 0 \\ 1 \\ 0 \end{bmatrix}$$

so that only goods x_1 and x_2 are consumed.

Then we have

$$\hat{B} = \begin{bmatrix} 2 & 1.8 \\ 1 & 1.8 \end{bmatrix}$$

$$\hat{p} = [1, 1]$$

$$w = c[1, 1]\begin{bmatrix} 2 & 1.8 \\ 1 & 1.8 \end{bmatrix}^{-1}$$

If the consumer's utility function gave a point like A' in Figure 3.8 on the z^2, z^3 facet, we would have

$$\hat{B} = \begin{bmatrix} 1.8 & 1 \\ 1.8 & 2 \end{bmatrix}$$

$$\hat{p} = [1, 1]$$

giving

$$w = c[1, 1]\begin{bmatrix} 1.8 & 1 \\ 1.8 & 2 \end{bmatrix}^{-1}$$

$$= c[\tfrac{1}{9}, \tfrac{4}{9}]$$

Note that a small change in p_3 does not affect the shadow prices on the $z^1 z^2$ facet, nor does a small change in p_1 affect the shadow prices on the $z^2 z^3$ facet. If, however, p_3 changed from 1 (as given) to $\tfrac{1}{2}$, the extreme points of the budget set become

$$x^1 = \begin{bmatrix} 1 \\ 0 \\ 0 \end{bmatrix}; \qquad x^2 = \begin{bmatrix} 0 \\ 1 \\ 0 \end{bmatrix}; \qquad x^3 = \begin{bmatrix} 0 \\ 0 \\ 2 \end{bmatrix}$$

giving

$$z^1 = \begin{bmatrix} 2 \\ 1 \end{bmatrix}, \qquad z^2 = \begin{bmatrix} 1.8 \\ 1.8 \end{bmatrix}; \qquad z^3 = \begin{bmatrix} 2 \\ 4 \end{bmatrix}$$

Since now $z^3 \gg z^2$, z^2 cannot be in E and the combinations along $z^1 z^2$ are no longer on a facet of the efficiency frontier.

We can summarize the properties of a facet optimum as follows:

(1) *It is attained by the consumption of exactly r goods.*

(2) *The marginal rates of substitution (in preference) between any two characteristics is equal to the ratio of the shadow prices of the characteristics.*

(3) *The relative shadow prices of characteristics are uniquely determined for each facet, the vector of shadow prices depending only on the prices of those goods which are associated with that facet. Thus the optimum is not affected by small changes in the prices of goods not relevant to the facet.*

3.7 Vertex Optima

If z^* is a vertex point, it is an extreme point and therefore corresponds to an extreme point of the budget set. Thus only one good is consumed.

No tangency equations exist, but certain inequalities must be satisfied. A vertex occurs either at the intersection of facets (as A or A' in Figure

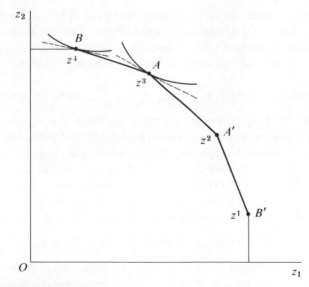

Figure 3.9. Vertex optima

3.9) or at the "end" of the efficiency frontier (B or B' in Figure 3.9).
It is obvious that the indifference surface $\{z \mid u(z) = u(z^*)\}$ must not
cut any of the facets which intersect at z^* and therefore that the slope
in any direction of the tangent plane to the indifference surface at z^*
is bounded by the slopes, in that same direction, of the relevant facets.
In two dimensions, as in Figure 3.9, the conditions are that the slope of
the tangent at A $\left(\dfrac{\partial u}{\partial z_1} \middle/ \dfrac{\partial u}{\partial z_2}\right)$ should be not greater than the slope
of facet $z^2 z^3$ and not less than the slope of facet $z^3 z^4$. In terms of shadow
prices:

$$(w_1/w_2)_{34} \leqq \frac{\partial u}{\partial z_1} \middle/ \frac{\partial u}{\partial z_2} \leqq (w_1/w_2)_{23}$$

For an "end" vertex (B or B' in Figure 3.9) one inequality relates
to the slope of the relevant facets, the other to the coordinate hyperplanes. In two dimensions the latter requires that the tangent does not
have a positive slope, which is automatically guaranteed by the assumed
property that $\dfrac{\partial u}{\partial z_i} > 0$, all i.

We shall consider the typical vertex optimum to be what might best
be called a strong vertex optimum, one in which the slope of the indifference surface is not equal to the slope of any of the relevant facets in any
direction. In two dimensions a strong optimum satisfies the strict
inequalities.

If we had, for example, $(w_1/w_2)_{34} = \dfrac{\partial u}{\partial z_1} \middle/ \dfrac{\partial u}{\partial z_2}$, giving an optimum at A
in Figure 3.9, A would be both a facet optimum (but not an interior
facet optimum) and a vertex optimum (but not a strong vertex optimum).
For more than two dimensions, the normal of the tangent hyperplane
to the indifference surface at z^* must have a slope "in between" the
slopes of the normals to the facets which meet in the vertex.

If $w^1, \ldots w^s$ are the shadow price vectors for the relevant facets,
they are also the direction vectors for the normals. The gradient vector
$\nabla u = \left[\dfrac{\partial u(z^*)}{\partial z_i}\right]$ is the normal to the indifference surface at z^*. Thus the
condition on the normals is equivalent to requiring that the positive
halfline (∇u) lie in the closed convex cone defined by the positive halflines $(w^1), \ldots (w^s)$.

In algebraic terms, this equivalent to requiring that u is a non-negative linear combination of the w's, that is

$$\nabla u = \sum \mu_i w^i: \quad \mu_i \geqq 0, \quad \text{all } i$$

If z^* is a strong vertex optimum, it lies in the interior of the cone, that is

$$\nabla u = \sum \mu_i w^i: \quad \mu_i > 0, \quad \text{all } i.$$

Since a strong vertex optimum requires only inequality relationships between the marginal rates of substitution in preference and the shadow prices on any of the relevant facets, such an optimum is not affected by small changes in any of the goods prices.

Thus we can sum up the properties of a *strong* vertex optimum:

(1) *It is attained by the consumption of only one good.*

(2) *The marginal rates of substitution in preference between pairs of characteristics are not equal to any ratio of shadow prices.*

(3) *The optimum is not affected by small changes in any of the goods prices.*

3.8   Edge Optima

The edge optimum has properties intermediate, in a sense, between those of a facet optimum and a vertex optimum. Since edges do not exist in two dimensions, we need to move to a three-characteristic model for illustration.

Figure 3.10 illustrates the efficiency frontier for four goods and three characteristics. The frontier consists of two triangular facets 123 and 124 (behind 123 in the diagram). The points 1, 2, 3, 4 are vertices corresponding to goods 1, 2, 3, 4 respectively. The two facets intersect along the edge 12, an edge of order 2.

It is clear that a consumer will be at an optimum at some point, like C, on edge 12 if and only if the tangent plane to the indifference surface at C (i) lies along the line 12; (ii) lies *outside* the feasible set everywhere except along 12.

We confine our attention to strong edge optima in which the tangent plane does not coincide with either 123 or 124.

If C is a strong edge optimum for a given consumer facing given prices, it is obvious that it will remain optimal for small changes in goods prices which pivot facet 123 or 124 (or both) around 12 as an

axis but will not remain optimal if the slope of the edge 12 is changed.
The consumer purchases goods 1 and 2 only.

A tangency condition is satisfied for an edge optimum since, in
Figure 3.10, the tangent to the indifference surface in the direction 12
must coincide with the edge 12. This condition cannot be expressed in
the usual simple terms since the direction 12 does not coincide with the
direction of any of the axes, and the condition requires that the ratio

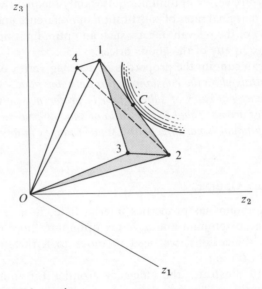

Figure 3.10. Edge optimum

of two linear combinations of marginal utilities be equal to the ratio
of the shadow costs of two linear combinations of characteristics.
As in the case of a facet optimum, an edge optimum is unaffected by
small changes in the price of any goods not relevant to that edge. A
good is not relevant to an edge if it does not correspond to a point
on any of the facets which intersect in the edge.

With more than three characteristics, we can have edges of various
orders. We shall not give a formal analysis of their properties, which
are analogous to those of the edge of order 2 in three-dimensional
C-space. We can summarize the leading properties of an edge optimum
of order k:

(1) *It is attained by the consumption of exactly k goods.*

(2) *The marginal rates of substitution between certain linear combinations of characteristics must equal the ratio of the costs of corresponding bundles of characteristics. A total of k − 1 such ratios must be equated.*

(3) *The optimum is unaffected by small changes in the prices of goods not actually consumed.*

3.9   Two-Stage Models

The analysis so far has been concerned with the simplest linear model in which goods are assumed to give rise directly to characteristics. The model can be given greatly increased adaptability by assuming that characteristics are derived from *consumption activities*, in which goods, singly or in combination, are the inputs.

Each activity is assumed to be linear and to require goods in fixed proportions so that the quantity of the kth good required to operate the jth activity at unit level is given by a fixed coefficient a_{kj}. We shall denote the level of the jth activity by y_j so that y is a vector giving the levels at which all the various activities are operated. The vector of goods will be denoted by x, as in the simpler model. Then the collection of goods required by the specified vector of activity levels is given by

$$x = Ay$$

The A matrix may be expected to contain some columns having only one non-zero entry, representing direct consumption of particular goods in the form of a one-good activities. Since activities, not goods directly, give rise to characteristics, the element b_{ij} of the B matrix now represents the amount of the ith characteristic derived from unit level of the jth activity, rather than unit quantity of the jth goods. Thus the characteristics collection associated with the activity vector y is

$$z = By$$

The consumption technology is now defined by the pair of matrices A, B. There may be any relationship between the number of goods (n), the number of activities (m), and the number of characteristics (r). A is of order $n \times m$, while B is of order $r \times m$.

Formally, the consumer's problem of choice under a linear budget constraint now has the form:

$$\text{Max } u(z)$$
$$\text{S.T.} \quad z = By \qquad y \geqq 0$$
$$x = Ay$$
$$px \leqq k$$

There are now *three* spaces: goods space, activity space, and character-istic space, instead of two. We could transform the problem into activity space:

$$\text{Max} \quad u(By)$$
$$\text{S.T.} \quad pAy = k$$

but shall find it convenient, as before, to continue to handle the analysis in characteristics space. The analysis is not, in fact, much more difficult than for the simpler model since we need deal only with activity space and characteristics space.

Given the goods price vector p, we note that $p_k a_{kj}$ is the value of the kth good incorporated into unit level of the jth activity. $\sum_k p_k a_{kj}$ $(= pA^j$, where A^j is the jth column of A) is the *unit cost* of operating the jth activity. From the A matrix and the vector goods prices we can, therefore, compute the vector of unit activity costs, $\pi = pA$, and use the budget constraint in activity space, $\pi y = pAy \leqq k$. This has the same general form as the budget constraint in goods space; that is, the boundary is a hyperplane.

Mapping out the feasible set in C-space involves only one simple extra step beyond those of the simple model. We proceed as follows:

(1) Compute the activity cost vector $\pi = pA$.

(2) Find the level at which each activity could be operated, if the whole budget were spent on inputs for that activity. For the jth activity, this level is given by k/π_j.

(3) Plot the characteristics collection corresponding to the operation of each activity at its maximum level as given by (ii). For the jth activity, this is the level $(k/\pi_j)B^j$, where B^j is the jth column of B.

(4) Form all convex combinations of the points plotted in (iii).

All the analysis and examples given for the simple model hold for the two-stage model, if we replace the word "good" by "activity," and "price of a good" by "cost of an activity." Activities will be efficient at low costs, inefficient at high costs. The simple model can be regarded as simply the special case in which each activity uses only one good, and each good is used in only one activity.

The analysis in this form will give efficient and optimal activity vectors rather than goods vectors. An optimal activity vector y^* must then be translated into goods. This is a simple matter, since we have the direct transformation

$$x^* = Ay^*$$

CHAPTER 4

DEMAND THEORY

4.1   End of the Representative Consumer

Demand theory in terms of the traditional model can be entirely carried out by considering a single "representative" consumer. By drawing a single suitable representative set of indifference surfaces we can describe the type behavior for any individual or any aggregate of consumers. This is because the traditional analysis is in terms of the special case of our more general model, in which the number of goods and characteristics is equal and the efficiency surface consists of a single facet.

In the more general model a single consumer can never "represent" the behavior of the market if the number of goods exceeds the number of characteristics. If there are, for example, eight goods and five characteristics, no single consumer will purchase more than five of the goods. Thus an observed market situation in which all eight goods are actually purchased cannot be "explained" by the behavior of a single representative consumer.

These observations follow, of course, from the analysis of the linear model given in Chapter 3. For at least some price changes the behavior of a consumer on one facet is not directly related to the behavior of the consumer on another, or that of a consumer on one vertex to that of a consumer on another, or even to that of a consumer on an adjacent edge or facet.

To describe total market demand we need, therefore, more than one representative consumer, at least one for every facet, vertex, and edge. Obviously, a consumer who chooses a point on one facet has, in some quite definite sense, different preferences from a consumer who chooses a point on another facet (or vertex or edge) under the same budget constraint. The relative demands for goods relevant to different facets will therefore depend on the relative purchasing powers of the consumers whose preferences lead to choice on the facets in question. Thus we see that the model set out in this work leads inevitably to a theory of demand in which variations among preferences rather than representative preferences determine the aggregate behavior of consumers.

Although we can discuss the behavior of a single consumer with certain preferences, we cannot, as in the traditional analysis, describe aggregate behavior (for a given income distribution) by simply taking a single representative consumer and multiplying his demand by the size of the market population. Aggregate demand cannot be analyzed without considering the distribution of preferences in relation to the distribution of income.

The inability to carry out a complete analysis in terms of the single representative consumer was the chief reason for choosing to discuss consumer choice subject to a budget constraint by mapping a utility function into goods space. The latter course would call for entirely different mappings for consumers on different facets, edges, or vertices. With eight characteristics and five goods, for example, the maximum number of possible facets is the number of ways in which five characteristics can be chosen from among eight, giving a potential of fifty-six different mappings to be considered, without taking account of edge or vertex consumers.

4.2   The Representative Efficiency Frontier

Although we cannot use a single representative consumer in our demand analysis, we can use a single representative efficiency frontier[1] so long

[1] It is in the universality and thus the "representativeness" of the efficiency frontier that we find the relationships that are shown to hold between the demands for various types of goods over widely differing markets. Although the analysis given here concentrates on the effects of price change on the efficiency frontier, the frontier is, of course, also determined by the technology. In some cases, the technical relationships may be such that feasible price ranges have little effect, and we have what are essentially *technical* demand relationships. Technical relationships can be of special importance in intertemporal choices. An important empirical finding relevant to this

as there is a linear consumption technology. Since the budget constraint on goods is linear, and the transformation from G-space to C-space is linear in this case, the efficiency frontiers for consumers with different incomes but facing the same prices will be geometrically similar and related by homogeneous expansion or contraction. If a consumer with unit income faces an efficiency frontier defined by extreme points (vertices) $x^1 \cdots x^m$, a consumer with income k will face an efficiency frontier defined by extreme points $kx^1 \cdots kx^m$, for the same prices and consumption technology.

We shall find it convenient to carry out most of our analysis with a single representative efficiency frontier, which will usually be for some convenient choice of unit income. The choice under budget constraint of a consumer with income k (> 1) is then established in the following ways:

(1) We "shrink" his preference map homogeneously in proportion $1/k$ so that his chosen point on the efficiency surface will have the proportions relevant to income k, not to the same consumer at income level 1.

(2) We allot him a market weight k so that his actual purchases will be k times those corresponding to the point on the unit efficiency frontier.

Figure 4.1 shows how consumers with incomes 1 and 2 are related to the same normalized efficiency surface. Figures 4.1(a) and 4.1(b) show the efficiency surfaces for the two consumers drawn in the "natural" sense. In Figure 4.1(b), $I_{2,1}$ and $I_{2,2}$ identify the indifference curves which consumer II can attain with incomes 1 and 2 respectively. In Figure 4.1(c), the efficiency surface is normalized for unit income. Consumer I's indifference curves are simply transferred from Figure 4.1(a). Those for consumer II are, however, shrunk in proportion $1/2$, giving new curves $I'_{1,2}$, $I'_{2,2}$. The chosen point appears as B', giving the same choice as B in Figure 4.1(b) after multiplying by the market weight of 2.

This apparently strange procedure is desirable in the present analysis because we have lost the representative consumer. By using the normalized efficiency surface we can relate the behavior of the large number of

---

is that the order in which durable goods are acquired (which good before which) is relatively constant over households. See J. Paroush, "The consumption technology and order relations in consumption." Unpublished dissertation, Columbia University, 1969.

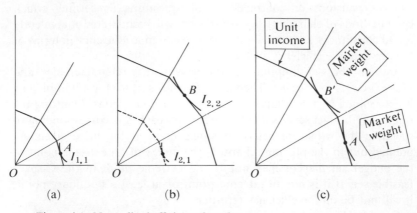

Figure 4.1. Normalized efficiency frontiers

different consumers who must now be considered. Note that the shrinking (or stretching, if $k < 1$) of the individual preference maps is necessary only insofar as the proportions in which a consumer chooses characteristics, at fixed prices, changes with income. For homogeneous (or homothetic) preferences we need consider only the market weight appropriate to each consumer since indifference curves for an individual are all related by simple expansion or contraction.

When we consider an aggregate of consumers it is apparent that the same effect on demand occurs whether, in Figure 4.1(c), the curve $I'_{2,2}$ is (i) the transformed (shrunk) indifference curve for a single consumer with income 2 or (ii) the "natural" indifference curve for each of two identical consumers with unit incomes.

Thus in analyzing aggregate demand in terms of a representative efficiency frontier, the relevant parameter associated with each indifference curve passing through a chosen point is simply its *market weight*. It does not matter whether this is derived from a large number of identical consumers with low incomes or a small number of identical consumers with high incomes.

The use of preference distributions and market weights will be treated at greater length in Chapter 5.

4.3 Efficiency Substitution

Since all consumers facing the same prices and consumption technology must choose from feasible sets which are related by homogeneous scalar expansions or contractions, all questions concerning which combinations of characteristics are efficient will be answered equivalently for all consumers. In other words, we can examine efficiency in terms of a representative efficiency surface.

Assume the consumption technology, with r characteristics and $n(> r)$ goods, to be given. Then the efficiency surface for a unit income is determined by the relative prices of the various goods. Omitting the origin, the budget set has n extreme points, each one corresponding to spending the whole budget on a single good at the price given. As pointed out in the previous chapter, the image of an extreme point of the budget set may or may not be an extreme point in the C-space feasible set. If it is not an extreme point or at least a boundary point, it will not be on the efficiency frontier.

Consider Figure 4.2, which gives a two-characteristic example. There are five goods, four of which are assumed to have prices that remain fixed and whose images in C-space are the points $G_1 \cdots G_4$. In the absence of the fifth good, all points $G_1 \cdots G_4$ are extreme points, and the efficiency surface is defined by these points and the line segments joining them.

The fifth good has a variable price. Its image in C-space will always be on the half line labeled G_5, being closer to the origin along this halfline when the price of the good is high, farther from the origin when the price of the good is low.

Now consider how the efficiency frontier changes when the fifth good is taken into account at various prices. Start with a relatively high price, which gives the point A in the figure. This point lies inside the frontier defined by $G_1 G_2 G_3 G_4$ and is clearly inefficient. At this price G_5 will not be purchased by any consumer (assuming all are efficient choosers), and the situation is just as though G_5 did not exist. The efficiency frontier is shown in Figure 4.3(a).

Let the price of G_5 fall so that its image point moves out along (G_5) to the point B, which is on the line segment joining G_2 and G_3. At this price purchase of G_5 is marginally efficient, in the sense that consumers can attain exactly same combinations of characteristics by spending their budget on G_5 or on combinations of G_5 and G_3 (for a point on segment BG_3) or of G_5 and G_2 (for segment BG_2), as on combinations of G_2 and G_3. The efficiency frontier, shown in Figure 4.3(b), is identical with that of Figure 4.3(a) except that there is now an option, which neither adds nor subtracts anything, of attaining certain points by purchasing G_5.

If the price of G_5 falls somewhat farther, to give point C in Figure 4.2, there is a change in the efficiency frontier. All points on G_2G_3 are now inefficient relative to point C or to points of CG_2 or CG_3. A new vertex, C, and two new facets, CG_2, CG_3, have replaced the facet G_2G_3 on the frontier, which is shown in Figure 4.3(c). The frontier now has four facets instead of three, with all five goods giving efficient points.

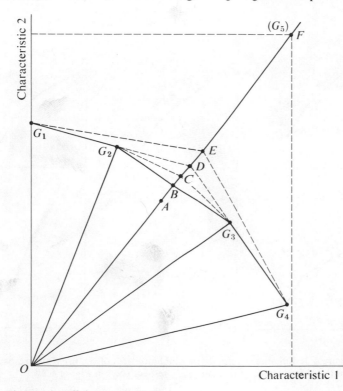

Figure 4.2. Efficiency substitution

A further fall in the price of G_5, to give point D in Figure 4.2, will cause a further change in the efficiency frontier. At this price all points on G_3G_4 become inefficient relative to points on DG_4. The three facets G_2C, CG_3, G_3G_4 are now replaced by two facets, G_2D and DG_4. Good G_3 no longer gives any point on the efficiency frontier and will no longer be purchased by any efficient consumer. The new frontier is shown in Figure 4.3(d).

Another fall in the price of G_5, to give point E, will make facets G_1G_2 and G_2D inefficient relative to points on G_1E, reducing the frontier to two facets, G_1E and EG_4, shown in Figure 4.3(e). Good G_2 has now dropped out.

Finally, if the price of G_5 falls sufficiently to give a point like F, the efficiency frontier degenerates into the single vertex F, since spending

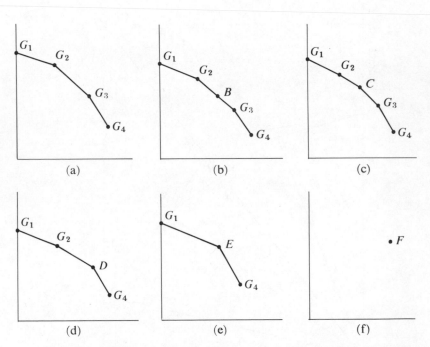

Figure 4.3. Efficiency frontiers for different prices of G_5. (a)–(f) correspond to frontiers when image of G_5 is at A–F, respectively, in Figure 4.2

the whole budget on G_5 gives more of all characteristics than can be obtained by spending on any combination of other goods. This final stage, of total *dominance*, can occur only if G_5 possesses something of all relevant characteristics. A good like G_1 in Figure 4.2, which has only one of the characteristics, could not be dominant, however low its price, the ultimate efficiency frontier for a very low price of G_1 would be a facet with the second vertex corresponding to one of the goods which possesses some of characteristic 1.

Although the simple example we have examined contains only two characteristics, it illustrates well enough how greatly the efficiency frontier can change when the prices of goods change sufficiently. If the prices of all five goods are varied in this example, any of the following efficiency frontiers can come into existence:

(1) Single-vertex frontiers with dominance by G_2, G_3, G_4, or G_5 [4 frontiers].

(2) Single-facet frontiers defined by any two of the goods [10 frontiers].

(3) Two-facet frontiers involving any three of the goods [10 frontiers].

(4) Three-facet frontiers, with any one of the goods inefficient [5 frontiers].

(5) A four-facet frontier.

Thus there are a total of thirty different frontiers in this simple example. For a larger number of characteristics and goods the number increases very rapidly.

If the number of characteristics is larger than the number of goods, the shape of the efficiency frontier also changes with relative prices, although this case cannot be illustrated in a simple diagram. Even with three characteristics and two goods, as in Figure 4.4, the frontier may be an edge like AB with both of the goods efficient, or single vertices like C or D with one good dominant.

As prices change sufficiently, the images corresponding to different goods move on and off the efficiency frontier. If all goods possess all characteristics, every good can be inefficient at a sufficiently high relative price and can be dominant at a sufficiently low relative price. Some modification of this general statement is necessary if all characteristics are not possessed by all goods. A good which does not possess all characteristics cannot be dominant, however low its price, while a good that possesses a characteristic not possessed by any other good cannot be inefficient, however high its price. In the traditional model every good possesses a characteristic not possessed by any other so that all goods remain on the efficiency frontier at all prices.

The movement of goods on or off the efficiency frontier as relative prices change involves substitution of a good for a combination of goods or a combination of goods for a particular good. This substitution is universal since it depends on the criterion of efficiency only, and does not depend in any way on the nature of individual preferences. We shall refer to this effect as the *efficiency substitution effect*.

In the simple linear model with which we are concerned at this stage, efficiency substitution involves discontinuous switching, a good changing from being efficient (some positive quantity demanded) to inefficient (zero demand), or vice versa, as price changes by a very small amount. A more continuous efficiency substitution effect occurs in multistage linear models.

We can prove formally that the efficiency substitution effect is sufficient to guarantee the convexity of demand on which the existence and

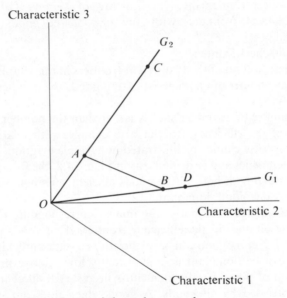

Figure 4.4. Three characteristics and two goods

stability of competitive equilibrium depend, although only in the weak sense. Nevertheless, this is an important result since the nature of the effect makes it completely independent of income distribution and of the convexity of individual preferences. This proof is embodied in the following theorem:

Even if characteristics are chosen in fixed proportions, demand will satisfy the convexity property $\Delta p_j \cdot \Delta x_j \leq 0$ when the price of only the jth good changes and income is adjusted so that the original collection can just be purchased at the new prices.

Let z^* be the characteristics chosen initially, with consumption technology matrix B and prices p^*. Then the goods collection $\bar{x}$ which is chosen will be the solution of the program.

$$\text{Min } p^*x$$
$$\text{S.T. } Bx = z^*, \quad x \geqq 0$$

Now let the prices become p^{**}. The new goods collection, x^{**}, to attain characteristics z^* efficiently will be the solution of

$$\text{Min } p^{**}x$$
$$\text{S.T. } Bx = z^*, \quad x \geqq 0$$

Since both programs have the same constraints, the solution of either program is feasible in the other. From the definition of a minimum in each program, this implies

$$p^{**}\bar{x} \geqq p^{**}x^{**}$$

and

$$p^*x^{**} \geqq p^*\bar{x}$$

If we multiply the constraint vector in a linear program by some scalar λ, the new solution vector is λ times the old, owing to the linearity of the problem. Thus the solution to the program

$$\text{Min } p^*x$$
$$\text{S.T. } Bx = \lambda z^*, \quad x \geqq 0$$

is $\lambda\bar{x}$. Choose λ so that

$$\lambda p^{**}\bar{x} = p^{**}x^{**}$$

From the first of the inequalities derived above, this implies that $\lambda \leqq 1$. The second inequality then implies

$$p^*x^{**} \geqq \lambda p^*x$$

with the equality only if $\lambda = 1$.

Write $x^* = \lambda\bar{x}$, then we have

$$p^{**}x^* = p^{**}x^{**}$$
$$p^*x^{**} \geqq p^*x^*$$

The first relationship expresses the fact that the income at prices $p^{**}(p^{**}x^{**})$ is just sufficient to buy the collection x^* at the new prices.

Subtracting the two relationships, we obtain

$$(p^{**} - p^*)(x^{**} - x^*) \leqq 0$$

a weak form of the generalized substitution effect. With $p_k^{**} = p_k^*$, $k \neq j$, we finally obtain

$$\Delta p_j \cdot \Delta x_j \leqq 0$$

4.4   Personal Substitution

In addition to the efficiency substitution effect, which is universal, there will generally be a *personal substitution effect* for an individual consumer. This effect is analogous to the substitution effect in the

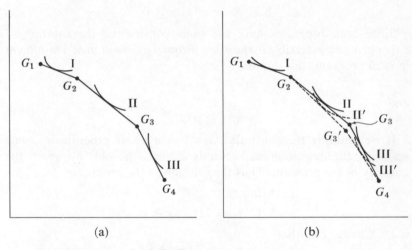

(a)   (b)

Figure 4.5. Personal substitution

traditional case and under the conditions of that case (each good uniquely associated with a single characteristic, and each characteristic with a single good) there is no efficiency substitution, all substitution being personal. Personal substitution depends on the consumer's personal preferences; hence the name. Broadly speaking, the extent of the personal substitution depends on (i) whether the consumer's initial choice was on a facet, edge or vertex; (ii) whether the price change is in a good relevant to the consumer's chosen point; and (iii) the convexity of the consumer's preferences.

The general situation is illustrated in Figure 4.5. We have a simple four-good two-characteristic consumption technology. Initially (Figure 4.5[a]) all goods are efficient, giving a three-facet frontier. A typical consumer is represented on each of the facets by indifference curves I, II, and III respectively.

Now let the price of G_3 fall by a small amount so that there is no change in efficiency but a slight change in the shape of the frontier from $G_1G_2G_3G_4$ in Figure 4.5(a) to $G_1G_2G_3'G_4$ in Figure 4.5(b). The slope of facet G_1G_2 is unaffected, since G_3 is not relevant to this facet, leaving the behavior of consumer I unaffected. But the slopes of G_2G_3' and $G_3'G_4$ differ from those of G_2G_3 and $G_3'G_4$. G_2G_3' is flatter than G_2G_3, and $G_3'G_4$ steeper than G_3G_4. If the indifference curves have the traditional smooth convexity, as drawn, there will be substitution effects, precisely analogous to those of the traditional analysis, for consumers II and III. These can be separated in the usual way from the income effects which arise because the efficiency frontier has been pushed forward. As to be expected, the substitution effects are such as to induce both consumers II and III to increase consumption of G_3 relative to G_2 and G_4, because the new chosen points (for the pure substitution effect) will be closer to G_3 on both facets than the old chosen points.

Although consumer I is unaffected by the price of G_3 as far as personal substitution is concerned, for small changes around the price configuration of Figure 4.5(a), a sufficiently large price fall could cause an efficiency substitution effect. For a sufficiently large fall in the price of G_3, the facets G_1G_2 and G_2G_3 would become inefficient relative to the new facet G_1G_3, and consumer I would switch from a combination of G_1 and G_2 to a combination of G_2 and G_3 to G_1 and G_3, so that consumers I and II would now be on the same facet. Thus efficiency changes result in a change in the context of personal substitution effects. For strict vertex consumers, illustrated in Figure 4.6, there would be zero personal substitution effect for a very small change in the price of G_3. Nor would there be a personal substitution effect for a consumer who chose characteristics in fixed proportions (point indifference curves).

We can give a more formal analysis of the private substitution effect by proceeding in the following way. In the previous section we consider a consumer interested in a specific characteristics collection z^* to be solving the following program, the solution of which we shall denote by x^*, rather than $\bar{x}$ as before:

$$\text{Min} \quad p^*x$$

$$\text{S.T. } Bx = z^* \qquad x \geqq 0$$

The dual of this program is

$$\text{Max} \qquad wz^*$$
$$\text{S.T. } wB \leqq p$$

The solution, w^*, satisfies the relationship

$$w^*a^* = p^*x^* = k$$

where k is income.

The vector w^* is, of course, the vector of shadow prices of characteristics for the consumer choosing characteristics collection z^*.

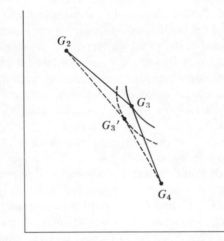

Figure 4.6. Vertex consumers

From a theorem in linear programming, the same shadow prices apply to all collections which give rise to the same basis, that is, to all collections on the same facet (or edge or vertex). We can, therefore, consider the consumer as locally maximizing $u(z)$ subject to the *characteristics budget constraint* $w^*z \leqq k$. Let $\hat{B}$ be the optimal basis in B. That is, $\hat{B}$ consists of those columns of B corresponding to the goods actually consumed to attain z^* efficiently. We shall confine ourselves to a facet consumer so that the number of goods consumed on the facet is equal to the number of characteristics, and $\hat{B}$ is a square non-singular matrix of order $r \times r$. If $\hat{p}$, $\hat{x}$ refer to subvectors concerning only those goods actually relevant to the facet in question, we have

$$w^* = \hat{p}^*\hat{B}^{-1}$$
$$z^* = \hat{B}\hat{x}^*$$

Now let the subvector of goods prices change from the original $\hat{p}^*$ to $\hat{p}^{**}$ so that we have

$$w^{**} = \hat{p}^{**}\hat{B}^{-1}$$

The vector w^{**} represents the shadow prices on the original facet at the new goods prices. If the original facet has become inefficient, the optimal solution will be on a new facet, with a new basis. We can consider w^{**} as representing *pseudo-shadow prices*, the shadow prices subject to an additional constraint that the consumer must choose on the original facet, whether it is efficient or not. *We deny him the opportunity of efficiency substitution.*

If we adjust the consumer's income so that he can just purchase the original characteristics collection z^* at the new pseudo-shadow prices w^{**}, his new characteristics collection will satisfy the *substitution theorem*

$$(w^{**} - w^*)(z^{**} - z^*) = 0$$

if his preferences are convex. Using the relationships between w, $\hat{p}$ and z, $\hat{x}$, we obtain

$$(w^{**} - w^*)(z^{**} - z^*) = (\hat{p}^{**} - \hat{p}^*)\hat{B}^{-1}\hat{B}(\hat{x}^{**} - \hat{x}^*)$$
$$= (\hat{p}^{**} - \hat{p}^*)(\hat{x}^{**} - \hat{x}^*)$$
$$= (p^{**} - p^*)(x^{**} - x^*)$$

since $x_i^{**} - x_j^* = 0$ for all x_j not in $\hat{x}$. Thus we have the *personal substitution effect*

$$(p^{**} - p^*)(x^{**} - x^*) = 0$$

for a price change and an income adjustment which enables the consumer to buy the old characteristics collection at the new prices without making any efficiency substitution.

Finally, we need to show that, if we permit efficiency substitution, the consumer is able to buy the original characteristics at the new shadow prices (not the pseudo-shadow prices, but the true shadow prices after full adjustment), if his income is adjusted so that he can just buy the original goods at the new goods prices. Let goods prices change from p^* to p^{**} and income be adjusted so that $p^{**}x^* = p^{**}x^{**}$, where x^* is the original, and x^{**} the final, goods collection. Let w^*, w^{**}; z^*, z^{**} be the original and final shadow prices and characteristics collections. Then from basic linear programming theory, we have

$$w^{**}z^{**} = w^*Bx^{**} = p^{**}x^{**}$$
$$w^{**}z^* = w^{**}Bx^* \leqq p^{**}x^*$$

But $p^{**}x^{**} = p^{**}x^*$, giving

$$w^{**}z^{**} \geqq w^{**}z^*$$

so that the original characteristics collection can certainly be purchased at the new shadow prices. *Thus the personal and efficiency effects cannot counteract each other but work in the same direction.*

4.5   Circles of Substitution

In this section we shall examine the effect of a change in the price of one good on the demand for other goods, drawing on both efficiency and personal substitution effects. Being interested in *aggregate effects*, we assume the existence of a large number of consumers with "well-distributed" preferences in the sense that, for every configuration of the efficiency frontier, there are consumers choosing points on every facet, edge, and vertex.

Consider Figure 4.7 (identical with Figure 4.2), which shows a five-good, two-characteristic model in which the prices of G_1, G_2, G_3, G_4 remain fixed while the price of G_5 changes. In terms of their "characteristic-1 intensity" the goods are in increasing order of the characteristic 1 to characteristic 2 ratio: G_1, G_2, G_5, G_3, G_4, that is, G_5 lies between G_2 and G_3 in this ratio. At a sufficiently high price, giving point A in the diagram, G_5 will be inefficient and will not be purchased at all. If the price falls to give point B (on the facet G_2G_3), G_5 is marginally efficient. Consumers on facet G_2G_3 will be indifferent in choosing between attaining their preferred point in this facet by combinations which include G_5, or combinations of G_2, and G_3 only. Demand will be a set, not a point. If any of G_5 is purchased at this price, it will be at the expense of G_2, G_3, or both. There will be no effect on G_1 and G_4.

A slight fall in the price of G_5, to a point like C, will now make the original facet G_2G_3 inefficient. This facet will be replaced on the efficiency frontier by the two facets G_2C, CG_3. No consumer previously on G_2G_3 will now purchase both G_2 and G_3 but will attain his chosen point on either G_2C or CG_3 by a combination of either G_5 and G_2 or G_5 and G_3. Thus as the price falls from that corresponding to A to that corresponding to C, there will be *efficiency substitution effects* causing a partial substitution of G_5 for both G_2 and G_3, in the aggregate. There will be no effect on the demand for G_1 and G_4.

A further small fall in the price of G_5 to give a point slightly beyond B

will result in *personal substitution effects* for consumers on G_2C and CG_3. These effects will be to substitute more of G_5 for G_2 and G_3. Such effects will continue as the price to G_5 falls further, until we reach point D. For a fall in price from a point just inside D to just beyond D, there will be another *efficiency effect*, as facets like CG_3 and G_3G_4 become

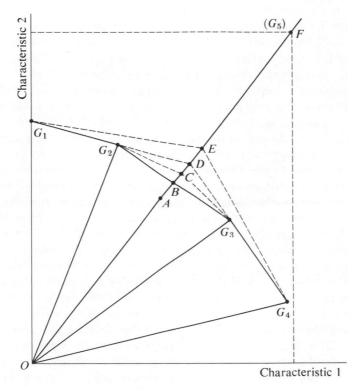

Figure 4.7. Circles of substitution

inefficient relative to the facet DG_4. At this price level G_3 becomes inefficient and will no longer be purchased, with the substitution of G_5 for G_3 having gone as far as it can. But now begins a substitution of G_5 for G_4, a good unaffected at the previous prices. Further fall in the price of G_3 will cause further substitution of G_5 for G_4, owing to personal effects. At a price corresponding to E, G_2 will cease to be efficient, and the substitution of G_5 for G_1 will commence. This will continue from personal effects as G_5 continues to fall in price. Final efficiency effects take place as the price of G_5 falls enough to make it dominate both G_1 and G_4, leaving G_5 as the only good purchased.

The process described above can be seen to consist of a series of stages in each of which substitution occurs from personal effects between the good whose price is falling and those efficient goods which are relatively close to it in the proportions of characteristics. In the transition from one stage to another efficiency effects result in those goods with characteristics proportions closest to the good whose price is falling becoming inefficient. The substitution process then moves out to cover the goods next closest in characteristic proportions, which were previously unaffected by the price fall. Thus we can describe the effect on other goods of a price fall in one good as consisting of ever-widening *circles of substitution*. For a small price fall only "close" goods are affected, but as the price continues to fall goods farther and farther away in terms of characteristics proportions will become affected.

This is an effect quite different from that of the traditional analysis, which presumes that substitution effects are spread among all other goods in a continuous manner. To generalize the analysis to r characteristics, let us consider the good whose price is falling (the *object good*) as giving an image on a halfline which is in the interior of a cone defined by some subset of r goods, the halflines corresponding to which form the generators of the cone. These r goods can be considered as *adjacent* or *zone 1 goods*. If the object good's price is initially high, so that the good is inefficient, the adjacent goods will define a *primary facet*. The zone 1 goods correspond to the vertices of the primary facet. They will also be the vertices of those other facets which meet the primary facet. Denote the goods corresponding to the vertices of this next ring of facets, excluding the zone 1 goods themselves, as *zone 2 goods*. We can continue to define successive zones of goods in an analogous fashion. Then the circles of substitution effect will be apparent in the following way:

(1) When the object good is just efficient, a small further price fall will affect the demand for zone 1 goods only.

(2) As zone 1 goods become inefficient (one at a time, unless there are special coincidences in the characteristics proportions), the substitution effects will spread to zone 2 goods (one at a time). When all zone 1 goods are inefficient, the substitution effects will influence the demand for all zone 2 goods.

(3) Further price falls will result in the effects spreading to zone 3 goods, and so on.

We can, therefore, determine the "closeness" of substitutes from the *consumption technology* and consider closeness of substitution an intrinsic effect, depending on objective characteristics of goods rather than on the nature of consumer preferences. The "closest" substitutes for the object good will be the zone 1 goods. Given the consumption technology, these goods can be determined, a priori. Although closeness of substitution can be regarded as independent of preferences, we may have to take account of prices in any operational context. Suppose, for example, that the prices of all zone 1 goods were so high that they were all inefficient relative to goods other than the object good. In other words, these goods would be inefficient, whatever the price of the object good. Then zone 2 goods would be the closest effective substitutes.

The shape of the personal preferences would affect the degree of substitution between the object good and zone 1 goods, since the substitution effects themselves are personal, but only the preferences of consumers who purchase all r zone 1 goods (consumers initially making choices on the primary facet) are relevant. That is, the prediction of the simple linear model is that, over a certain price range, the cross elasticity relative to the price of the object good is non-zero for zone 1 goods and zero for other goods. The size of the cross elasticity depends on preferences.

4.6   Pure Income Effects

If an individual consumer's income increases, with prices held constant, his feasible set in C-space undergoes a scalar expansion with no change in shape. He is now able to attain characteristics collections previously infeasible and can reach a higher indifference level than before.

In our analysis the effects of a pure income charge will be initially in terms of characteristics. Although a pure income change will leave the shape (but not the scale) of the efficiency frontier unchanged, the consumer's chosen point on his new frontier will not necessarily be the scaled-up equivalent of his original chosen point. It will depend on how the shapes of his indifference curves change as we move out from the origin, just as it does in traditional analysis when the indifference curves are drawn in goods space. Given the way in which a consumer's preferred characteristics collections vary with income, holding prices and the technology constant, the way in which his goods collection varies with income can be deduced.

In the traditional analysis it is usual to describe the effect of pure income changes on goods in terms of income elasticities—the ratio of the proportionate change in the quantity of a good to the proportionate change in income, prices being constant. For general purposes broad descriptive terms such as "luxury good" (income elasticity greater than unity), "essential good" (income elasticity less than unity but non-negative), "inferior good" (income elasticity negative) are widely used.

We can give analogous terms to characteristics (and indeed compute income elasticities of characteristics) so that we may have "luxury" and "essential" characteristics. In a simple two-characteristics model one characteristic will be a "luxury" characteristic, the other an "essential" characteristic, unless preferences are homogeneous and both characteristics have unit income elasticity.

Can we have "inferior" characteristics analogous to inferior goods? Not within the context of the simple linear model. An inferior characteristic would have to be one that was positively desired up to some income level, then negatively desired. We shall discuss, in a later chapter, satiation effects that lead to such a switch in the relationship of characteristics to people, but here we shall confine ourselves to characteristics that are always positively desired. This does not mean that there will be no inferior goods in our simple model. To make this quite clear, we can assert the following:

A good may be inferior even though all of the characteristics it possesses are positively desired.

The point can be demonstrated easily by the following example, in which there are two goods and two characteristics, with the simple technology matrix

$$\begin{bmatrix} 2 & 1 \\ 1 & 2 \end{bmatrix}$$

and both goods have unit prices.

Suppose the initial income to be 10, giving the efficiency frontier G_1G_2 shown in Figure 4.8. The consumer chooses point $C(11, 19)$ on the frontier, corresponding to consumption of 1 unit of G_1 and 9 units of G_2. Income is now doubled, with prices constant, to give the new frontier $G_1'G_2'$. The consumer's preferred point is now $C'(38, 22)$,

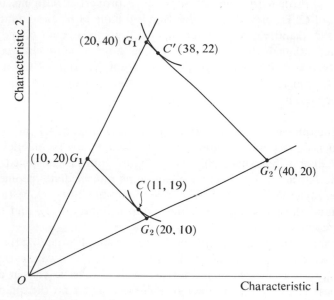

Figure 4.8. Inferior goods

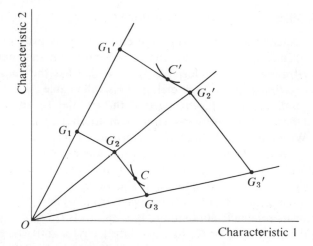

Figure 4.9. Three goods and two characteristics

clearly consistent in terms of preference properties with his original choice of C. The new goods collection is 9 units of G_1 and 1 unit of G_2. Thus the quantity of G_2 has fallen by 8 units as a result of the rise in income, although the consumer obtains more of both characteristics at C' than at C. It is obvious, of course, from the example and from the general properties of the situation, that the inferior good must necessarily be less intensive in the luxury characteristics than the non-inferior good.

In the three-good case the analysis is richer. Figure 4.9 shows a case in which G_3 (the inferior good) is consumed at low income levels but not at all at high income, while G_1 (a luxury good) is consumed at high income but not at low income. Over some intermediate income range the consumer switches from G_2-G_3 combinations to G_2 alone (a vertex optimum, thus sustained for some finite income range), and then to G_1-G_2 combinations.

Having clarified the inferior good case, we simply note that the choice of characteristics as income changes can vary in any way, except that more positively desired characteristics will always be chosen at high incomes. The consequent effect of income changes on the quantity of any one good can be of any kind, including a decline in quantity with increase in income.

4.7   The Income Effects of a Price Change

If all characteristics are positively desired a fall in the price of any one good, with money income unchanged, will push out that part of the efficiency frontier in characteristics space which has the image of the good in question as one of its vertices. This will enable consumers who choose points on the relevant part of the frontier to attain a more preferred position, with effects equivalent to that of a pure income change. With more goods than characteristics, a small fall in the price of any one good will not, of course, give any income effect to consumers not originally consuming (or on the margin of consuming) that good. In the 5-good, 2-characteristic case shown in Figure 4.10, a small decline in the price of G_3 to shift its image from G_3 to G_3' has no effect on consumers originally choosing points on facets G_1G_2 or G_4G_5.

The fall in the price of G_3 has two effects: (i) it shifts facets G_2G_3, G_3G_4 outwards, giving an income effect; (ii) it changes the slope of facets G_2G_3 and G_3G_4, giving personal substitution effects. Thus, just

as in the Slutsky-Hicks analysis in the traditional case, we can separate
the effect of a price change into income and personal substitution
effects. We can also carry out the traditional hypothetical experiment
in which the consumer's income, after the price change, is adjusted to
enable him just to attain his original indifference curve by optimal
choice (giving the pure substitution effect), and then the income is
restored to its original level (giving the pure income effect).

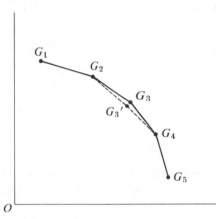

Figure 4.10. Income effect

A sufficiently large change in the price of a good may introduce
efficiency substitution effects, which may affect an individual who was
not originally a consumer of the good in question. In terms of circles
of substitution (see earlier in this chapter) a small price change in the
object good will have income effects only on a consumer choosing a
point on the primary facet. Large price changes which cause efficiency
substitution effects will result in income effects spilling over into zone 2
goods and thus to persons not originally consuming the object good. It
is obvious, of course, that the income effects cannot spread beyond zone
1 consumers unless efficiency substitution effects occur.

CHAPTER 5

THE DISTRIBUTION OF PREFERENCES

5.1 A Simple Model of Preference Distribution

The properties of aggregate demand depend, in the characteristics model, on variations in preferences so that we cannot describe aggregate behavior in terms of a single representative consumer and must concern ourselves with the distribution of different preferences over the whole population. It is clearly a task of hopeless magnitude to attempt to describe the possible distributions of preferences in any general sense. Any single individual's preferences are constrained, on standard assumptions, only by convexity and monotonicity, and the preference maps of different individuals may differ in any way, provided only that the basic properties hold for each individual.

As an exploratory device, therefore, it is useful to set up a simple model of preference distribution. Such a model should have the following properties:

(1) The preferences of any individual should satisfy traditional assumptions as to monotonicity and convexity of preferences.

(2) Preferences should be expressible in simple functional form.

(3) The functional form should be the same for all individuals, variations being characterized by variations in coefficients or parameters of the functions.

A simple model possessing these properties is that based on Cobb-Douglas preference functions, with each indifference curve having the form (for r characteristics):

$$\prod_{i=1}^{r} z_i^{\alpha_i} = \text{constant}, \qquad \sum \alpha_i = 1$$

An individual preference function is defined by some choice of the indices, α_i, so that different preferences correspond to different choices of the α_i's. The distribution of preferences over the population can then be described by the distribution of α_i's.

To reduce the model to its simplest form, we shall consider a world of only two characteristics. Then we have:

(1) For any individual, the indifference curves are defined by:

$$z_1^{\alpha} z_2^{1-\alpha} = \text{constant } (0 \leqq \alpha \leqq 1)$$

(2) Preference variation is defined by a variation in α, so we have only a single parameter whose distribution need be considered. We shall refer to α as the preference parameter. At the extremes, a consumer for whom $\alpha = 0$ is interested only in z_2, one for whom $\alpha = 1$ is interested only in z_1.

A Cobb-Douglas preference function has two special properties which inhibit its use in a representative consumer model of the traditional kind:

(a) It is homogeneous, giving unit income elasticities for both goods.

(b) It has unit elasticity of substitution, so that the proportion of total income spent on each good depends only on the parameter α and is unchanged with changes in relative prices or incomes.

These properties imply such highly special results for demand theory in the traditional setting that the Cobb-Douglas form is inappropriate for traditional representative consumer analysis. Somewhat greater generality can be obtained by using the CES functional form in this case, but elasticities of substitution are still constant. As a preference function for an individual consumer in a spectrum of preferences, these specialized properties are of less concern since the properties of aggregate demand are determined by the distribution of the preference parameter as well as the properties of the individual functions. As we shall see, all we really imply by the Cobb-Douglas form is that a given consumer's preferences fit this general form at each utility level. We do not require that a particular individual have the same preference parameter at different utility (or income) levels.

5.2   Income Distribution

Consider all consumers with the same preferences, that is, the same value of α. Since we are still assuming a linear consumption technology, the feasible set in C-space is the same for all consumers, except for scalar expansion or contraction. Since the Cobb-Douglas function is homogeneous, all consumers with the same α will choose equivalent points on their efficiency frontiers, that is, points which transform into each other by scalar expansion or contraction of the feasible set in proportion to income. This is illustrated by the equilibrium conditions for the individual, which are expressed entirely in terms of proportions and slopes. It follows that for two consumers with the same α, one with income λ times that of the other, characteristics will be chosen in the same proportions, one consumer choosing exactly λ times as much of each characteristic as the other consumer. Because of this linearity, total consumption of characteristics (hence of goods) for all consumers with the same α will be proportional to the aggregate income of those consumers and independent of the distribution among those consumers.

Aggregate choice will, on the other hand, be influenced by the distribution of income between consumers with different α's. We can postulate a distribution of income in terms of α, so that $\phi(\alpha)$ gives the average income of those consumers whose preference parameter has the value α. If we consider the feasible set in C-space to be drawn for unit income, we can locate the characteristics collection that will be chosen by a consumer with a given α and with unit income. The total characteristics (and the goods giving rise to them) for all consumers with preference parameters between α and $\alpha + d\alpha$ will then be given by the product of the number of consumers and average income of those consumers. Let us call this the *aggregate market weight $dW(\alpha)$* for persons with preference in this range. Then we have

$$dW = \phi(\alpha) \cdot f(\alpha)\, d\alpha$$

Since all predictions of aggregate demand depend only on dW and not on the number of individuals concerned, we can, in many cases, simply use a combined distribution,

$$\psi(\alpha) = \phi(\alpha) \cdot f(\alpha)$$

instead of individual distributions for preferences and income.

In some cases we may wish to distinguish the preference and income distributions and may even wish to make one depend on the other. We can handle income-biased preferences in this way. Suppose, for example, that z_1 was a "luxury" characteristic so that persons with high incomes were more interested in z_1 than those on low incomes with "equivalent" preferences. For simplicity, assume all incomes are identical, then all rise in the same proportion. Because "special interest" in z_1 is equivalent to a high value of α we can deal with this case by treating the preference distribution as a function of average income over all consumers, with the relationship such that the distribution is skewed more toward high values of α as income increases. A simple model of this kind would be

$$f(\alpha) = a + bk\alpha$$

This is skewed (linearly) toward high values of α, the degree of skewness being determined by the constants a, b, and the average income level k.

Note that, although the individual preference function is homogeneous, we can take care of a variety of income effects by building them into the preference distribution. This is, in effect, equivalent to assuming that the preference parameter of a given individual is not constant but varies with income. In other words, once we are concerned with aggregate market behavior, we do not need to associate a particular value of the preference parameter permanently with a particular individual or group of individuals but merely with a particular individual at a specific income level. The aggregate model "sees" no difference between having individuals with preference parameters which remain constant with income (homogeneous preferences), but having income distribution varying, and maintaining a constant proportionate distribution of income while individual parameters vary with income. Thus the homogeneity of the Cobb-Douglas preference function, which is a major obstacle to its use for the traditional representative consumer, presents no equivalent problems when we have a preference distribution analysis.

5.3   Individual Equilibrium Conditions

For a *facet* of slope, $-m$, an individual consumer will choose a point on the facet at which

$$\frac{dz_2}{dz_1} = -m$$

where dz_2/dz_1 is taken along an indifference curve. We have

$$\frac{dz_2}{dz_1} = - \frac{\alpha}{1 - \alpha} \frac{z_2}{z_1}$$

Thus the consumer will choose a point on the facet for which

$$\frac{z_2}{z_1} = \frac{1 - \alpha}{\alpha} m$$

provided such a point exists.

Since a facet will not typically extend from the z_1 axis to the z_2 axis, there will be values of α for which the ratio z_2/z_1 given by the above

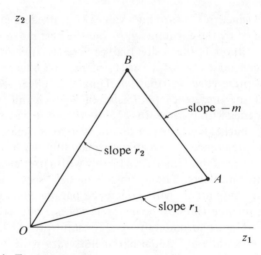

Figure 5.1. Facet consumers

expression cannot be attained on the facet. Suppose the facet is AB in Figure 5.1. Denote the slope of OB by r_2 and the slope of A by r_1. Then a consumer whose preferences are defined by a particular value of α will reach equilibrium on this facet only if the ratio z_2/z_1 at which the indifference curve has slope $-m$ lies between the ratios r_1 and r_2. Thus this consumer will have an optimum on facet AB if and only if

$$r_2 \gneqq \frac{1 - \alpha}{\alpha} m \gneqq r_1$$

After simple manipulation, this is equivalent to

$$\frac{m}{m + r_2} \leqq \alpha \leqq \frac{m}{m + r_1}$$

We can now state the condition for a *facet consumer*.

For a facet with slope $-m$, *the slopes of the rays from the origin to whose terminal points are* r_1, $r_2(r_2 > r_1)$, *a consumer with indifference curves* $z_1^\alpha z_2^{1-\alpha} = $ *constant will choose a point on that facet if and only if*

$$\frac{m}{m + r_2} \leqq \alpha \leqq \frac{m}{m + r_1}$$

Consider a particular vertex which is the intersection of facets with slopes $-m$, $-m_2(m_1 > m_2)$ and such that the slope of the ray from the origin to the vertex is r. For a consumer on this vertex, $z_2/z_1 = r$, and the slope of the tangent to the indifference curve at this point is given by

$$\frac{dz_2}{dz_1} = - \frac{\alpha}{1 - \alpha} r$$

The consumer will choose the vertex as optimal if and only if dz_2/dz_1 lies between the slopes of the adjacent facets, that is, if

$$m_1 \geqq \frac{\alpha}{1 - \alpha} r \geqq m_2$$

This gives

$$\frac{m_1}{r + m_1} \geqq \alpha \geqq \frac{m_2}{r + m_2}$$

Thus:

For a vertex at the intersection of facets with slopes $-m_1$, $-m_2(m_1 > m_2)$, *the slope of the ray through the origin to which is* r, *a consumer with indifference curves* $z_1^\alpha z_2^{1-\alpha} = $ *constant will choose that vertex if and only if*

$$\frac{m_1}{m_1 + r} \geqq \alpha \geqq \frac{m_2}{m_2 + r}$$

For an *end vertex*, we have either

$$1 \geqq \alpha \geqq \frac{m}{1 + r} \quad \text{(lower end vertex)}$$

$$\frac{m}{m + r} \geqq \alpha \geqq 0 \quad \text{(upper end vertex)}$$

where $-m$ is the slope of the facet at whose termination the end vertex lies.

Given any efficiency frontier, and a consumer for whom α has some particular value, the above rules enable us to locate the vertex or facet on which the consumer's chosen characteristics collection will lie.

5.4   The Distribution of Choices

We are now in a position to introduce preference distribution. Let $F(\alpha)$ be the cumulative distribution function so that $F(\alpha)$ gives the number of consumers whose preference parameters lie between 0 and α. The density function is $f(\alpha) = F'(\alpha)$ so that

$$dF = f(\alpha)\, d\alpha$$

gives the number of consumers whose preference parameters lie between α and $\alpha + d\alpha$. Then the total number of consumers who will choose a particular vertex, or a point on a particular facet, is given by:

(a) For a facet:

$$\int_{\frac{m}{m+r_2}}^{\frac{m}{m+r_1}} f(\alpha)\, d\alpha$$

(b) For a vertex:

$$\int_{\frac{m_2}{m_2+r}}^{\frac{m_1}{m_1+r}} f(\alpha)\, d\alpha$$

(c) For an end vertex:

$$\int_{0}^{\frac{m}{m+r}} f(\alpha)\, d\alpha \qquad \text{or} \qquad \int_{\frac{m}{m+r}}^{1} f(\alpha)\, d\alpha$$

It is obvious that, since every facet is terminated by its intersection with another facet or by an end vertex, and every vertex is an end vertex or the intersection of two facets, the total number of consumers is given by

$$\int_{0}^{\frac{m_1}{m_1+r_1}} f(\alpha)\, d\alpha + \int_{\frac{m_1}{m_1+r_1}}^{\frac{m_1}{m_2+r_2}} f(\alpha)\, d\alpha + \int_{\frac{m_1}{m_1+r_2}}^{\frac{m_2}{m_2+r_2}} f(\alpha)\, d\alpha + \cdots = \int_{0}^{1} f(\alpha)\, d = F(1)$$

so that the count is exhaustive.

5.5   The Rectangular Distribution Model

The simplest possible preference/income distribution model is one in which we assume:

(1) Uniform distribution of income so that average income is constant over α.

(2) Rectangular distribution of preferences, with constant density (which we can take to be unity), so that $f(\alpha) = 1$.

We shall turn to explore the properties of this distribution. Since $f(\alpha) = 1$, we have immediately:

$$\text{No. of consumers on facet} = \frac{m}{m + r_1} - \frac{m}{m + r_2}$$

$$= \frac{m(r_1 - r_2)}{(m + r_1)(m + r_2)}$$

$$\text{No. of consumers on vertex} = \frac{m_1}{m_1 + r} - \frac{m_2}{m_2 + r}$$

$$= \frac{r(m_1 - m_2)}{(m_1 + r)(m_2 + r)}$$

Intuitively, the rectangular distribution gives in some sense, a "uniform" distribution of preferences. This uniformity property is expressed in the following important result:

If there is a rectangular preference distribution, consumers are distributed uniformly along any facet, in the sense that the line density along the facet is constant.

Consider a facet with slope $-m$, terminated by vertices A, B such that the slopes of OA, OB are r_1, r_2 respectively, with $r_2 > r_1$. Such a facet was shown in Figure 5.1. Since all results are independent of scale, let us put the z_1 (horizontal) coordinate of B equal to unity. Then it is easily seen that the coordinates of the vertices A, B are:

$$A: \left[\frac{m + r_2}{m + r_1}, r_1 \left(\frac{m + r_2}{m + r_1} \right) \right]$$

$$B: [1, r_2]$$

Take some point C on this line segment AB such that $BC/AB = \lambda$.

This point will have coordinates

$$\frac{\lambda r_2 + (1 - \lambda)r_1 + m}{m + r_1}, \frac{m[\lambda r_1 + (1 - \lambda)r_2] + r_1 r_2}{m + r_1}$$

The slope of the ray OC will be

$$\rho = \frac{m[\lambda r_1 + (1 - \lambda)r_2] + r_1 r_2}{\lambda r_2 + (1 - \lambda)r_1 + m}$$

A consumer will choose point C on the facet if his indifference curve is tangent at that point, that is, if his preference parameter is such that

$$\rho = z_2/z_1 = \frac{1 - \alpha}{\alpha} m$$

We can eliminate ρ between the above relationships and solve for α in terms of λ, to obtain

$$\alpha = \frac{m[(r_2 - r_1)\lambda + (m + r_1)]}{(m + r_1)(m + r_2)}$$

Now the line density along AB is $f(\lambda)$, given by

$$f(\lambda) = f(\alpha) \frac{d\alpha}{d\lambda}$$

$$= \frac{m(r_2 - r_1)}{(m + r_1)(m + r_2)} \qquad \text{since } f(\alpha) = 1$$

This is constant along the facet.

Using this result, we can derive another of importance:

If there is a rectangular preference distribution and uniform distribution of income, the aggregate expenditure over all consumers on any facet will be equally divided between the two goods which correspond to the vertices terminating the facet.

Each vertex terminating the facet is an extreme point of the feasible set in C-space and therefore the image of an extreme point in G-space. An extreme point in G-space corresponds to expenditure of the total income on a single good. Now consider the facet AB and a consumer choosing point C on AB such that $BC/AB = \lambda$. Such a consumer spends a proportion λ of his income on the good corresponding to B, and a proportion $(1 - \lambda)$ on the good corresponding to A. If a rectangular preference distribution is assumed with unit density, and average income for consumers with given α as k, the aggregate market weight associated with the segment of the facet between C and a point close to it is:

$$dW = \phi(\alpha)f(\alpha)\frac{d\alpha}{d\lambda}\,d\lambda$$

$$= k\frac{m(r_2 - r_1)}{(m + r_1)(m + r_2)}\,d\lambda$$

The expenditure on the goods corresponding to B, A will be $\lambda\,dW$, $(1 - \lambda)\,dW$ respectively. Aggregate expenditure on the goods by all consumers on the facet will then be given by:

Good corresponding to B:

$$\int_0^1 \lambda\frac{dW}{d\lambda}\,d\lambda = k\frac{m(r_2 - r_1)}{(m + r_1)(m + r_2)}\int_0^1 \lambda\,d\lambda$$

$$= \tfrac{1}{2}k\frac{m(r_2 - r_1)}{(m + r_1)(m + r_2)}$$

Good corresponding to A:

$$\int_0^1 (1 - \lambda)\frac{dW}{d\lambda}\,d\lambda = \tfrac{1}{2}k\frac{m(r_2 - r_1)}{(m + r_1)(m + r_2)}$$

Since the aggregate income of all consumers on the facet is equal to average income multiplied by the number of consumers, giving

$$k\frac{m(r_2 - r_1)}{(m + r_1)(m + r_2)}$$

the proposition is proved.

5.6 The Rectangular Distribution in the Traditional Case

The traditional consumer model is, of course, a special case of the general linear model in which the number of goods is equal to the number of characteristics, with each good having only one characteristic and each characteristic being derived from only one good. Thus the efficiency frontier in C-space has a single facet, terminating on the two axes. With a rectangular preference distribution and uniform income distribution, the previous result shows that aggregate expenditure will be divided evenly between the two goods, at all prices and incomes. Thus the rectangular distribution, in the traditional case, gives the same prediction as we would obtain from a single representative consumer with indifference curves

$$z_1^{1/2} z_2^{1/2} = \text{constant}$$

and income equal to the aggregate income of all consumers. This is not a surprising result. A model using a single representative consumer of this kind would not, of course, give the same results as the distributed preference model for cases other than those that correspond to the traditional model.

5.7 Simple Numerical Examples

Consider the numerical example used earlier, with the following specifications:

$$B = \begin{bmatrix} 2 & 1.8 & 1 \\ 1 & 1.8 & 2 \end{bmatrix}$$

$$p = \begin{bmatrix} 1 & 1 & 1 \end{bmatrix}$$

Assume rectangular distribution of Cobb-Douglas preferences, with density 100 and uniform income distribution with unit average income. The geometry of the efficiency frontier is identical with that shown in Figure 5.2.

Computation of aggregate demand depends on the various ratios of the form $m/m + r$. The relevant ratios are:

$$R_1 = \frac{m_1}{m_1 + r_1} = 0.889$$

$$R_2 = \frac{m_1}{m_1 + r_2} = 0.800$$

$$R_3 = \frac{m_2}{m_1 + r_2} = 0.200$$

$$R_4 = \frac{m_2}{m_2 + r_3} = 0.111$$

The distribution of consumers over the efficiency frontier is then given

by:
$$\text{Facet } z^1z^2 : 100[R_1 - R_2] = \quad 8.9$$
$$\text{Facet } z^2z^3 : 100[R_3 - R_4] = \quad 8.9$$
$$\text{Vertex } z^1 : 100[1 - R_1] \quad = \quad 11.1$$
$$\text{Vertex } z^2 : 100[R_2 - R_3] = \quad 60.0$$
$$\text{Vertex } z^3 : 100[R_4 - 0] \quad = \quad 11.1$$
$$\overline{ 100.0}$$

The heavy bunching of consumers on vertex z^2 is due to the relatively sharp angle at the vertex. The symmetry of the distribution is implicit

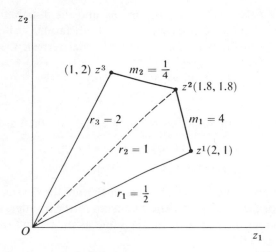

Figure 5.2. Vertex consumers

in the symmetry of the consumption technology and the preference distribution. Since all consumers have unit income, and since purchases by facet consumers are evenly divided between the goods corresponding to the end points of the facet, we can calculate the expenditure distribution.

Distribution of Expenditure

Good 1	(Vertex $z^1 + \frac{1}{2}$ Facet z^1z^2)	15.5
Good 2	(Vertex $z^2 + \frac{1}{2}$ Facet $z^1z^2 + \frac{1}{2}$ Facet z^2z^3)	69.0
Good 3	(Vertex $z^3 + \frac{1}{2}$ Facet z^2z^3)	15.5
		100.0

Prices being unity, the above figures show quantities as well as expenditures.

Effect of Price Variation

(*1*) *Change in Price of Good 2.* If p_2 increases from 1 to $1 + \delta p_2$ (with δp_2 small), the amount of good 2 that can be purchased with unit income will decrease from 1 to $1 - \delta p_2$, neglecting second-order terms. The coordinates of the vertex z^2 on the efficiency frontier will then become

$$[1.8(1 - \delta p_2), \ 1.8(1 - \delta p_2)]$$

This will affect the facet slopes m_1 and m_2 and the distribution of consumers over all three vertices as well as both facets. Using standard approximation methods (ignoring second-order terms), the new facet slopes are

$$m_1 = 4(1 - \tfrac{4.5}{4}\delta p_2)$$
$$m_2 = \tfrac{1}{4}(1 + \tfrac{4.5}{4}\delta p_2)$$

The changes in the ratios $R_1 - R_2$ given earlier are then as follows:

(1) $-1.111\delta p_2$ (3) $+1.8\delta p_2$
(2) $-1.8\delta p_2$ (4) $+1.111\delta p_2$

From these we obtain the changes in the number of consumers on each vertex or facet. Owing to the symmetry of the frontier, the number of consumers on vertex z^3 will be the same as on z^1, and on facet z^2z^3 the same as on z^1z^2:

Facet z^1z^2	$+68.9\delta p_2$
Facet z^2z^3	$+68.9\delta p_2$
Vertex z^1	$+111.1\delta p_2$
Vertex z^2	$-360.0\delta p_2$
Vertex z^3	$+111.1\delta p_2$
	$000.0\delta p_2$

The effect of the price change is to reduce the number of consumers on vertex z^2 and increase them on the other two vertices and both facets. These shifts are entirely due to the change in slope of the two facets, which shifts some consumers from z^2 on to the facet, and some facet consumers on to the end vertices z^1 and z^3.

We can easily compute the change in expenditures and in quantities:

	Expenditure Changes	Quantity Changes
Good 1	$+145.6\delta p_2$	$+145.6\delta p_2$
Good 2	$-291.1\delta p_2$	$-360.0\delta p_2$
Good 3	$+145.6\delta p_2$	$+145.6\delta p_2$

Expenditure on good 2 falls by less than the fall in the number of consumers on vertex z^2 because of the increase in facet consumers, half of whose expenditures will be on good 2. The quantity change for good 2 is larger than the expenditure change because of the price increase.

Using the original quantities given earlier, we can compute the (uncompensated) price elasticities at $p_1 = p_2 = p_3$:

$$\eta_{22} = -5.2$$
$$\eta_{12} = \eta_{32} = +9.3$$

where η_{ij} is the elasticity for the ith good with respect to the jth price.

Note that we obtain relatively high elasticities, although the elasticity associated with a single Cobb-Douglas preference function in the traditional setting is only -1. The substitution in the present model is largely due to the shifts of consumers between vertices and facets.

(2) *Change in Price of Good 1.* An increase in the price of good 1 will have an asymmetric effect, since it changes the slope of facet z^1z^2 only. The effect of an increase in p_1 from 1 to $1 + \delta p_1$ will be as follows, computed in a similar manner as previously:

Distribution of Consumers

(Change in number of consumers)

Facet z^1z^2	$-68.9\delta p_1$
Facet z^2z^3	0
Vertex z^1	$-111.1\delta p_1$
Vertex z^2	$+180.0\delta p_1$
Vertex z^3	0

	Expenditure Changes	Quantity Changes
Good 1	$-145.5\delta p_1$	$-161.0\delta p_1$
Good 2	$+145.5\delta p_1$	$+145.5\delta p_1$
Good 3	0	0

The price elasticities are

$$\eta_{11} = -10.4$$
$$\eta_{21} = +2.1$$
$$\eta_{31} = 0$$

Demand Curves for Good 2

By taking $p_1 = p_3 = 1$ and considering various values of p_2, we can compute the coordinates of z^2 for each price, the corresponding values of m_1 and m_2, and ultimately the quantities of good 2. The resulting demand schedule is shown in Table 5.1 and the demand curve in Figure 5.3.

Table 5.1   Demand and Expenditure Schedule for Good 2
Uncompensated: average income unity, $p_1 = p_3 = 1$

Price	Expenditure	Quantity	Comment
≤ 0.9	100	$100/p_2$	Dominant at these prices
$0.9(1 + \varepsilon)$	$100(1 - 1.5\varepsilon)$	$111(1 - 2.5\varepsilon)$	$\eta = -2.5$
0.95	83.2	87.6	
1.00	69.0	69.0	$\eta = -5.2$
1.05	56.2	53.5	
1.10	41.3	37.5	
1.15	30.0	26.1	
$1.20(1 - \varepsilon)$	$16.7(1 + 15\varepsilon)$	$13.9(1 + 16\varepsilon)$	$\eta = -16*$
>1.20	0	0	Dominated at these prices

* At $p_2 = 1.20$, z^2 falls on facet $z^1 z^3$, which becomes efficient at this stage. At this price consumers using good 2 will be indifferent to the choice between it and some combination of goods 1 and 3. Consequently expenditure on good 2 at $p_2 = 1.20$ may lie anywhere between 0 and 16.7. The elasticity $\eta = -16$ at $p_2 = 1.20(1 - \varepsilon)$ jumps discontinuously to $\eta = -\infty$ as p_2 passes through the value 1.20. Price 1.20 maps into the *set* $\{q \mid 0 \leq q \leq 13.9\}$.

Demand Curve for Good 1

Good 2 was shown to have two dominance phases. At any price below 0.9 it dominates both G_1 and G_3, while at any price above 1.20

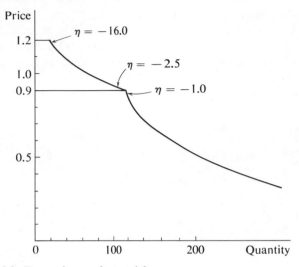

Figure 5.3. Demand curve for good 2

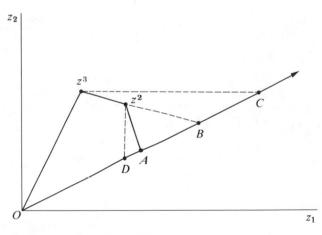

Figure 5.4. Dominance phases of good 1

it is dominated by combinations of G_1 and G_3. The prices of G_1 and G_3 were held constant at unity throughout.

If we now keep the prices of G_2 and G_3 constant at the unit level and vary the price of G_1 to map out the demand curve for G_1, we find three dominance phases, illustrated in Figure 5.4. Vertices z^2, z^3 in the figure correspond to the characteristics obtained by spending the whole budget on G_2, G_3, respectively, with $p_2 = p_3 = 1$. The position of vertex z^1

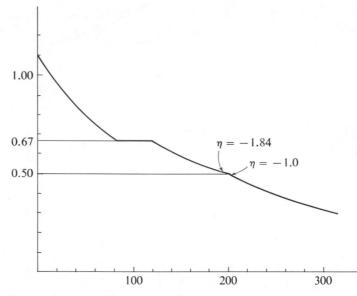

Figure 5.5. Demand curve for good 1

depends on p_1. At a low enough value of $p_1(\leq 0.5)$ z^1 lies beyond the point $C[4, 2]$ and G_1 dominates both G_2 and G_3. In the next range $(0.5 \leq p_1 \leq 0.67)$, z^1 lies between C and the point $B[3, 1.5]$ so that combinations of G_1 and G_2 dominate G_3. There is no dominance if z^1 falls between B and the point $D[1.8, 0.9]$, corresponding to the price range $0.67 \leq p_1 \leq 1.11$. For $p_1 > 1.111$, z^1 lies closer to the origin than D, and G_1 is dominated by G_2. The demand curve for G_1 is shown in Figure 5.5, with representative points of the demand schedule given in Table 5.2.

Table 5.2   Demand and Expenditure Schedule for Good 1
$p_2 = p_3 = 1$, unit average income, rectangular preference distribution

Price	Expenditure	Quantity	Comment
$\leqq 0.5$	100	$100/p_1$	Dominant, $\eta = -1$
$0.5(1 + \varepsilon)$	$100(1 - 0.84\varepsilon)$	$200(1 - 1.84\varepsilon)$	$\eta = -1.84$
$0.67(1 - \varepsilon)$	$78(1 + 0.92\varepsilon)$	$116(1 + 1.92\varepsilon)$	$\eta = -1.92$
$0.67(1 + \varepsilon)$	$60(1 - 1.36\varepsilon)$	$90(1 - 2.36\varepsilon)$	$\eta = -2.36$
0.95	21.9	23.1	
1.00	15.6	15.6	$\eta = -10.4$
1.05	8.4	8.0	
$1.11(1 - \varepsilon)$	1.5ε	1.35ε	$\eta = -\infty$
1.11	0	0	Dominated by G_2

Note. There are discontinuities in the elasticities at prices 0.5 and 0.67. The demand relationship $q = q(p)$ is not a simple function but a point-to-set mapping, since the quantity associated with $p = 0.67$ is any point in the set $\{q \mid 90 \leqq q \leqq 116.2\}$. At $p = 0.5$ the quantity has the unique value 200, although there is a discontinuity in the shape of the curve.

5.8   Skewed Distributions

Since the aggregate market weight is the product of the income density and the preference density, skewness in income distribution with rectangular preference distribution gives similar results to skewness in preference distribution with uniform income distribution. We shall assume uniform income distribution and consider skewness in the preference distribution. The complexity of the mathematics is the chief limitation, so we shall consider only a linearly skewed distribution of the kind

$$f(\alpha) = a + b\alpha$$

Since the general linearly skewed distribution is the sum of a rectangular distribution with density α, and a purely skewed distribution with density $b\alpha$, we can simplify by treating only the purely skewed portion here. Thus we shall consider only

$$f(\alpha) = b\alpha$$

The total number of consumers is given by

$$\int_0^1 f(\alpha)\, d\alpha = \tfrac{1}{2} b$$

It is convenient to normalize this for a total population of 1, giving

$$f(\alpha) = 2\alpha$$

Since $f'(\alpha) > 0$, the distribution is skewed toward high values of α, that is, toward greater aggregate interest in z_1 relative to z_2 than in the rectangular case. Then the number of consumers on a vertex with radius vector slope r, at the intersection of two facets with slopes $-m_1$, $-m_2$, is:

$$\int_{\frac{m_2}{m_2+r}}^{\frac{m_1}{m_1+r}} 2\alpha\, d\alpha = \left(\frac{m_1}{m_1 + r}\right)^2 - \left(\frac{m_2}{m_2 + r}\right)^2$$

with corresponding expressions for facets.

This simple skewed distribution poses no computation problems, since we simply square the ratios R_1–R_4 given earlier, then take the differences between the squares rather than between the ratios. Taking the previous numerical example (with unit prices for all goods), we can compute the population distribution for a total population of 100. The results, with those for the rectangular distribution as comparison, are given in Table 5.3.

The number of consumers on vertex z^2 is the same as on the skewed and non-skewed distribution because this vertex is exactly in the center of the distribution. The distribution of *expenditure* between goods

Table 5.3   Distribution of Consumers

	Number of Consumers	
	Skewed Distribution $f(\alpha) = 2\alpha$	Rectangular Distribution $f(\alpha) = 1$
Facet $z^1 z^2$	15.0	8.9
Facet $z^2 z^3$	2.8	8.9
Vertex z^1	21.0	11.1
Vertex z^2	60.0	60.0
Vertex z^3	1.2	11.1
	100.0	100.0

corresponding to the end points of a facet will no longer follow the simple rule of equal division, as in the rectangular case. For a point on a facet which divides it in proportions λ, $(1 - \lambda)$, we have, as before,

$$\alpha = \frac{m[(r_2 - r_1)\lambda + (m + r_1)]}{(m + r_1)(m + r_2)}$$

In the neighborhood of such a point the market weight is

$$dW = f(\alpha) \frac{d\alpha}{d\lambda} d\lambda \qquad \text{(since the income distribution is uniform)}$$

$$= 2\alpha \frac{d\alpha}{d\lambda} d\lambda$$

$$= 2 \frac{m[(r_2 - r_1)\lambda + (m + r_1)]}{(m + r_1)(m + r_2)} \frac{m(r_2 - r_1)}{(m + r_1)(m + r_2)} d\lambda$$

$$= 2 \left\{ \left[\frac{m(r_2 - r_1)}{(m + r_1)(m + r_2)} \right]^2 \lambda + \frac{m^2(m + r_1)(r_2 - r_1)}{(m + r_1)^2(m + r_2)^2} \right\} d\lambda$$

Thus the expenditure on the good corresponding to r_1 (we shall refer to this as G_1) will be

$$(A\lambda^2 + B\lambda) \, d\lambda = \tfrac{1}{3}A + \tfrac{1}{2}B$$

and on G_2, the good corresponding to r_2:

$$[A\lambda(1 - \lambda) + B(1 - \lambda)] \, d\lambda = [-A\lambda^2 + (A - B)\lambda + B] \, d\lambda$$
$$= -\tfrac{1}{3}A + \tfrac{1}{2}(A - B) + B$$
$$= \tfrac{1}{6}A + \tfrac{1}{2}B$$

where

$$A = \left[\frac{m(r_2 - r_1)}{(m + r_1)(m + r_2)} \right]^2$$

where

$$B = \frac{m^2(m + r_1)(r_2 - r_1)}{(m + r_1)^2(m + r_2)^2} = \frac{m + r_1}{r_2 - r_1} \cdot A$$

It is easily verified that the total expenditure $\tfrac{1}{2}A + B$ is equal to $\left(\dfrac{m}{m + r_1}\right)^2 - \left(\dfrac{m}{m + r_2}\right)^2$, the total income of consumers on the facet.

The ratio of expenditures on the two goods can be simplified to

$$\frac{\text{Expenditure on Good 1}}{\text{Expenditure on Good 2}} = \frac{3m + 2r_2 + r_1}{3m + 2r_1 + r_2}$$

$$= 1 + \frac{r_2 - r_1}{3m + 2r_1 + r_2}$$

Unlike the rectangular case, this distribution of expenditure depends on all the properties of the facet, since m, r_1, r_2 all occur within it.

Table 5.4   Distribution of Expenditure

	Skewed Preference Distribution $f(\alpha) = 2\alpha$ ($\times$ 100)	Rectangular Preference Distribution $f(\alpha) = 1$ ($\times$ 100)
Good 1	29.1	15.5
Good 2	68.3	69.0
Good 3	2.6	15.5
	100.0	100.0

However, it will not be greatly different from distribution in the rectangular case, since $r_2 - r_1$ will be small compared with $(3m + 2r_1 + r_2)$. Using this result in our example, the relative expenditures on the two facets are

Facet $z^1 z^2$ $G_1/G_2 = 13/11$
Facet $z^2 z^3$ $G_2/G_3 = 17/16$

giving, as expected, more expenditure on the good with the higher ratio of characteristic 1 to characteristic 2, although the divergence from even splitting of expenditure is not large. The expenditures (= quantities, since price are unity) on the various goods are shown in Table 5.4.

5.9   The Skewed Distribution in the Traditional Model

If we have a single facet with $r_1 = 0$, $r_2 = \infty$, application of the previous formula on expenditure distribution shows that the ratio of expenditure on G_1 to expenditure on G_2 is 2:1, whatever the slope of the facet. This is equivalent to the behavior of a single representative consumer with indifference curves

$$z_1^{2/3} z_2^{1/3} = \text{constant}$$

No matter what we do with the distribution in the traditional model, the result is always equivalent to the behavior of a single representative consumer with Cobb-Douglas preferences. The elasticity of demand is always unity.

CHAPTER 6

EXTENSIONS AND MODIFICATIONS

6.1 Negative Characteristics

If a characteristic is such that the *universal* reaction to it is negative—that is, everyone would prefer less of this characteristic to more of it, other things being equal—it is more convenient to take the negative of the characteristic. This calls for a negative coefficient in the appropriate place in the technology matrix (if the good possesses the characteristic in positive quantity) but maintains the ordinal superiority of collections having more characteristics (including more of the negatives of negative characteristics) and leaves the efficiency definitions unchanged.

The aim of the sign change is to preserve the traditional sense of order in characteristic space (increasingly preferred positions for movements to the northeast), and its usefulness depends on universal negative reaction by consumers. A good or activity may possess the characteristic in a negative or positive amount. One activity (food and sleep may produce "energy," for example, while another, work, may absorb it). If characteristic Z, measured in the natural sense, is possessed positively by one activity and negatively by another, we reverse all signs if this characteristic is a negative characteristic in our sense. We are still assuming that characteristics, whether negative or positive, are linearly related to goods or activities and are combinable.

With negative characteristics, we are no longer confined to the non-negative orthant in characteristics space, but the shape and sense of indifference loci are the same as with positive characteristics only. Both diagrams of Figure 6.1 show the feasible set in C-space for two characteristics where one of these (z_2) is a negative characteristic. Typical indifference curves have been drawn in, using the sign change discussed above. In Figure 6.1(a) the technology is such that both activities possess positive amounts of both characteristics, giving a feasible set lying entirely outside the non-negative quadrant. In Figure 6.1(b), on

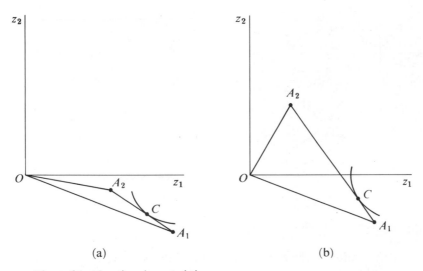

Figure 6.1. Negative characteristics

the other hand, A_2 is assumed to have negative amounts of z_2, giving a feasible set lying partly in the non-negative quadrant and partly outside it. The indifference curves, giving preferred collection C, have been drawn to illustrate the point that the preferred position is not necessarily in the non-negative quadrant even if the feasible set lies partly in this quadrant. For the case shown in Figure 6.1(a), a typical technology matrix would be

$$B = \begin{bmatrix} 3 & -2 \\ 2 & -1 \end{bmatrix}$$

while for the case shown in Figure 6.1(b), a typical matrix would be

$$B = \begin{bmatrix} 3 & -2 \\ 1 & 1 \end{bmatrix}$$

When the above sign convention is used, the analysis of situations with negative characteristics is basically the same as that of positive characteristics in characteristics-space itself. The shapes of efficiency frontiers and the nature of efficiency and private substitution effects are unchanged in terms of characteristics analysis, and the ordinal superiority of any point to those points to the southwest of it (in the two-characteristic case) is unchanged.

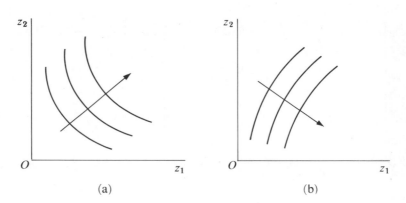

Figure 6.2. Positive and negative reactions to a characteristic

Preservation of the general structure of the analysis by a sign change is possible only for characteristics which are universally negative. If a characteristic is such that some react to it negatively, some positively, or such that a particular individual reacts positively at certain income levels and negatively at others (as in the case of the satiation effects discussed in Chapter 9), we are presented with a major problem because the efficiency criteria are no longer universal.

Consider a two-characteristic universe in which one characteristic (z_2) is positive to some consumers, negative to others, the other characteristic being universally positive. Then the indifference map of a consumer to whom z_2 is positive will have the traditional pattern shown in Figure 6.2(a). The indifference map of a consumer to whom z_2 is a negative characteristic, however, will look like Figure 6.2(b), and the two types of consumers will have quite a different view of the relative efficiency of different points in the feasible set. The arrows in the diagrams show the general direction of movement towards more preferred situations—northeast in Figure 6.2(a) as normally assumed but southeast in Figure 6.2(b).

Consider the feasible set shown in Figure 6.3, with three goods and two characteristics. For consumers to whom both characteristics are positive, G_3 is dominated by G_1 and only the facet G_1G_2 (including its vertices) is efficient. A typical preferred point for such a consumer will be C_1. For consumers to whom z_2 is a negative characteristic, however,

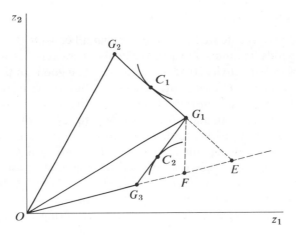

Figure 6.3. Efficiency substitution with mixed reactions to a characteristic

it is G_2 which is dominated by G_1, and the facet G_1G_3 which represents the efficiency frontier, so that a typical choice for such a consumer would be C_2.

Efficiency choices, and efficiency substitution, still exist, but they differ between the two groups of consumers, eliminating the universality of some efficiency effects. In the example given G_3, at a price sufficiently low to give its image at or beyond E in Figure 6.3, will dominate both G_1 and G_2 for all consumers. For a price which puts this image between E and F, combinations of G_1 and G_3 are still efficient for all consumers. But if the price of G_3 rises so that the image point lies closer to the origin than F, G_3 remains efficient to those consumers for whom z_2 is a negative characteristic and is, in fact, undominated by G_1 for these consumers at all prices. Thus, although there may be a sharp fall-off in demand as G_3 becomes inefficient for consumers viewing z_2 positively, the demand does not drop to zero as in our standard analysis.

Whether to adopt the sign change technique when there are divided reactions to a given characteristic is a matter of choice on an ad hoc basis. If the distribution of preferences was such that most consumers viewed the characteristic negatively, it would presumably be convenient to change its sign and represent the dominant behavior of the market by diagrams drawn with the traditional northeast preference ordering.

6.2   Characteristics as Inputs

In our analysis to date we have assumed that all consumption activities use only goods as inputs and produce only characteristics as outputs, as in the simplest activity, that of consuming one good. In this case the mapping from goods space into characteristics space is only in the forward direction. The introduction of negative characteristics, however, has laid the foundation for movement to more complex activity situations. If an activity produces a positive amount of a negative characteristic, we change the sign so that the activity now produces a negative amount of a desired characteristic (the relative absence of an undesired one), and it is then a short step to viewing the negative output of the characteristic as an input. We can view work, or sport, as either producing negative "energy," or as requiring "energy" as an input.

Some activities can be considered as taking place entirely in characteristics-space. If we regard "time" and "energy" as characteristics—for purposes of illustration only, since it is impossible to construct truly realistic models on the basis of no more than two characteristics—then sleep can be regarded as an activity using time as an input and producing energy as an output. For many purposes, there is no need to distinguish between a characteristic as an input into an activity, and as a negative output from that activity. The net output (z) of all characteristics from a given collection (y) of activities is given by

$$z = By$$

where the coefficient b_{ij} will be negative if the ith characteristic is regarded either as a negative output of, or as an input into, the jth activity. If there are no constraints on choice other than the budget constraint, no distinction is required between inputs and negative outputs. The optimizing problem has the same structure in both cases.

It is convenient, however, to consider characteristics specifically as inputs whenever there are non-budget constraints on these. If we regard "time" as a characteristic and time is an integral part of a consumption activity, it is appropriate to regard it as an input, rather than a negative output, because it is a primary input, limited in amount, that must be supplied entirely or mainly by the consumer. If time is the kth characteristic, the consumer is subject to the non-budget constraint $z_k \leqq \bar{z}_k$ (where $\bar{z}_k$ is the maximum time available to the individual—24 hours per day), in addition to his budget constraint. Time, or some characteristic expressing the same general property, is not the only input-characteristic of this kind. "Energy," or some equivalent, is also limited to the consumer, but, unlike time, the limits might perhaps be stretched by certain activities, such as sleeping or taking "pep pills."

It is not necessarily appropriate to consider an input into a consumption activity as a characteristic just because it is not a "good" in the traditional sense. Our analysis makes the distinction between goods and characteristics primarily on the basis that goods are directly obtained in the market, while characteristics are the direct object of preference. Suppose, for example, that "time" is such that (i) it cannot be obtained directly through the market; (ii) it is an input into many consumption activities; and (iii) it does not appear directly in the preference function. That is, a consumer has no direct interest in how time-consuming an activity is, although he may be interested in how the time used for one activity constrains his ability to engage in others. Then it would be inappropriate to regard "time" as a characteristic in our sense. It would be a *non-market input*, subject to constraints additional to any market constraints. If there were no effective constraints on the input we could simply ignore it completely as we would a free good.

6.3   Labor, Leisure, and Occupational Choice

The use of the characteristics approach enables us to view labor-leisure and occupational choices as more complex decision processes than is implied in the traditional analysis. We can, in particular, take account of both desirable and undesirable characteristics associated with work, instead of merely regarding it as an activity with a single input (time) and a single output (income). The simple examples given here are representative of the type of analysis that can be used in this area. For a realistic analysis we would need to go beyond the two dimension of the examples.

Work can be viewed as an activity that gives characteristics—some positive, some negative—and the commodity labor which is sold in exchange for goods. This is structurally equivalent to assuming some of the columns of the B matrix to have both negative and positive elements, corresponding to activities that "use up" some characteristics (or produce them in negative quantities) and produce others. In a work activity the corresponding column of the A matrix will contain a single negative coefficient for the commodity labor or, more differentiated, for one or more types of labor. If a work activity corresponds to a column of mixed signs in the B matrix, it is a recognition of the obvious truth that some work activities give rise to valued characteristics directly from the work itself.

Consider a very simple model of two characteristics with two commodities, labor and consumption goods. Both labor and consumption goods correspond to separate activities giving rise to the two characteristics in different proportions—perhaps negative in the case of labor. With no income other than labor, and only one good available to exchange for labor, we can collapse work and consumption into a single work-consumption activity. Given the wage rate in terms of the consumption good, the characteristics resulting from the work-consumption activity are given by a linear combination of the characteristics from work and consumption separately, the weights in the combination being given by the wage rate. Add another activity, leisure, which gives rise to the two characteristics, and the constraint that the weighted sum of the levels of activity labor and activity leisure is a constant. The model is illustrated in Figure 6.4. W represents a work-consumption activity giving positive levels of both characteristics, L represents a leisure activity, also giving positive levels of both characteristics. The constraint on total time (so that a linear combination of W and L is a constant) is represented by some line joining W, L.

If the constraint line has a negative slope like AB in the diagram, then individual consumer's utility functions will be tangent to the constraint at different points (like M, M'), and we shall have a neoclassical type of labor-leisure choice in which the proportions depend on individual preferences. Some consumers' preferences may be such that they will choose A (maximum work) or B (maximum leisure), but it is a private choice.

In this model, however, for a certain level of the wage, given the coefficients of the technology, the constraint may have a positive slope as in $A'B$ or AB'. If the constraint is $A'B$ (corresponding *ceteris paribus*, to a sufficiently low real wage), all individuals will choose B, the only efficient point on the constraint set $OA'B$. At a sufficiently high wage,

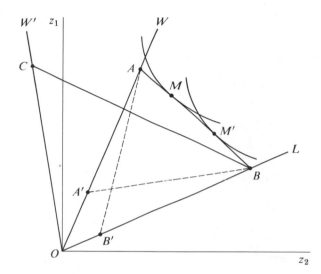

Figure 6.4. Labor and leisure

giving constraint set OAB', A, the maximum labor choice, is the only efficient choice and will be chosen by all individuals.

The above effect, in which for some wage range there is a private labor-leisure choice between efficient points while outside the range all individuals will take maximum work or maximum leisure, can occur only if both the work-consumption and leisure activities give both characteristics in positive amounts. If the using up of characteristic z_2 in labor exceeded the amount of that characteristic gained by consumption, the work-consumption activity might lie outside the positive quadrant, like W'. In this case a constraint like $A'B$ can exist, but not one like AB'. Furthermore, if the consumer will choose only positive characteristics vectors, no consumer will choose maximum work.

This model of the labor-leisure choice, which provides for objective and universal efficiency choices as well as private choices, may be the basis for a useful working model for an underdeveloped area. If the "leisure" be defined as "working one's own field," the work-consumption activity as entering the market economy, we see that there will be wages below which no peasant will offer himself as paid labor and that is an efficiency choice and not a private choice.

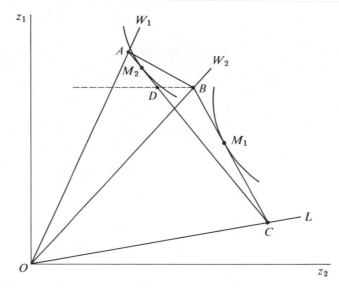

Figure 6.5. Occupational choice

We can use the same type of model also to analyze occupational choice. Suppose that we have two types of work (occupations) but otherwise the conditions are as above. If and only if the characteristics arising from the work itself are different in the two occupations, the two work-consumption activities will give rise to activities in different combinations. If the work characteristics are in the same proportion, the characteristics of the work-consumption activity will be in the same proportions and one or the other occupation will be the only efficient way to achieve this characteristic bundle.

Figure 6.5 illustrates one possible set of relationships for such a model. In the diagram, W_1, W_2 represent the characteristics combinations from work-consumption activities in occupations 1 and 2, L the characteristics combinations from leisure as an activity. The frontier consists of the lines AC (combinations of W_1 and leisure) and AB (combinations of W_2 and leisure). We shall impose the realistic restriction that an individual can have only a single occupation so that AB is not a possible combination of activities.

The choice of occupation, given the relationships in the figure, depends on personal preferences, being M_1 (combination of W_2 and leisure) for an individual with preferences skewed towards z_2 and M_2 for an individual with preferences skewed towards z_i. But note a special effect. For some individuals whose indifference curves cannot touch BC but can touch AC, the efficient choice will be the corner solution M_2 ($= B$). There is, in fact, a segment of AC to the left of W_2 (the part of AC to the right of W_2 is dominated by BC), lying below the horizontal through B which is inefficient relative to B and will never be chosen.

In a configuration like the above we have the very interesting effect where those who choose occupation 1 will work very hard at it; leisure-lovers will choose private combinations of occupation 2 and leisure, surely a good description of effects actually observed. The loss to certain individuals from confinement to a single occupation is obvious. Could he choose a combination of occupations 1 and 2, the individual at M_2 would do so and be better off than with a combination of occupation 1 and leisure. In a two-characteristic, three-activity model, of course, two activities will be chosen at most so that leisure plus both occupations will not appear.

The configuration in the diagram (Figure 6.5) represents the situation for some set of technical coefficients and specific wages in the two occupations. A large number of other configurations is possible. In particular, if the wage rate in occupation 2 fell sufficiently, BC would lie inside AC and occupation 2 would cease to be chosen by any individual. All individuals, in this case, would choose their various personal combinations of occupation 1 and leisure.

Confinement to a single occupation need not result in a welfare loss, even when neither occupation dominates the other in an efficiency sense. If the technical coefficients were different, so that the characteristics vectors representing occupation 2 and leisure changed places, the work-leisure combinations would be given by AB and BC, both efficient relative to any combination of occupations 1 and 2. In this case all individuals would optimize by some combination of leisure and any one of the occupations.

Approaches similar to those outlined above seem to provide a better basis for analysis of occupational choice than the traditional, non-operational, catch-all "non-monetary advantages."

6.4   Short-Term Intertemporal Effects

The range of this book has been set to exclude major problems of intertemporal choice. This is not because our model is not well adapted to extension in this direction (on the contrary, it is extremely useful in this context) but because a whole new ball game would be opened up. In particular, we cannot investigate intertemporal problems in a major way without an extensive analysis of intertemporal preferences. For the static analysis we can do well enough with the broadly accepted static preference assumptions of traditional analysis. Intertemporal preference analysis requires stronger assumptions, which do not have the same breadth of acceptance as the static assumptions.

The analysis given here is designed to illustrate the intertemporal properties that may be inherent in the technical goods-characteristics relationships, rather than a complete analysis of intertemporal choice. We shall simply assume here that:

(1) Characteristics vectors are dated relative to the time period at which decisions are made, so that $z^1 \cdots z^n$ represent characteristics vectors associated with the present and future periods.

(2) The characteristics vector which is relevant to decisions is the vector $\hat{z}$, of which the vectors at particular dates ($z^1 \cdots z^n$) are partitions. That is, present decisions are based on present and prospective characteristics collections. The preference function can be considered in the form $U(\hat{z})$, where U represents prospective utility.

(3) The complete goods vector $\hat{x}$, which includes immediate and prospective goods, is related to the complete characteristics vector by the consumption technology

$$\hat{z} = \hat{B}\hat{x}$$

All vectors and matrices are presumed to be ordered in such a way that, if there are m goods and N time periods, then $\hat{z}_1(\hat{x}_1)$ represents the amount of the first characteristic (good) in the first period, $\hat{z}_{m+1}(\hat{x}_{m+1})$ the amount of the first characteristic (good) in the second period, and so on.

We can, as in the static version, use the technology relationship to substitute for $\hat{z}$ in the utility function $U(\hat{z})$ and obtain prospective utility as a function of goods. As in the static version, however, we bury the relatively simple structure of the technology in the more complex structure of the utility function. In both cases it is more revealing to examine the structure of the technology separately, since efficiency effects can be analyzed without use of the properties of the utility function.

The simplest structure that we might impose on $\hat{B}$ is that of complete decomposability into the form

$$\begin{bmatrix} B & O & O & O & \cdots & O \\ O & B & O & O & \cdots & O \\ O & O & B & O & \cdots & O \\ \cdots & \cdots & \cdots & \cdots & \cdots & B \end{bmatrix}$$

so that $z^n = Bx^n$ for all n. This structure would imply that goods gave rise to characteristics only in their own period and that the prospective relationship between goods and characteristics is the same for all periods. In this case the efficiency choice for each period (the choice of the goods collections which are efficient for a given collection of characteristics) is independent of the choice for other periods.

The completely decomposable structure is, however, a special case. It is more interesting to consider the possibility of a structure which was not completely decomposable, but block triangular of the form

$$\begin{bmatrix} [B_1] & &] \\ O & [B_2] &] \\ O & O & [B_3] \end{bmatrix}$$

This structure implies that goods consumed in one period may give rise to characteristics in a later period as well as in their own. The zero submatrices to the left imply that there can be no characteristics before the goods are consumed, an assumption that might be relaxed for certain special cases.

Although this structure might be interpreted as related to consumer durable or capital goods, these are best treated in a more elaborate model in which activities using goods in combination, rather than single goods, give rise to the characteristics. The structure here is especially adaptable to the analysis of an aspect of consumer behavior that does

not fit the traditional analysis at all. That is of the good that is physi-
cally consumed in one period but gives rise to characteristics over several
subsequent periods.

Why do people spend a considerable part of their annual income on a
vacation which lasts only a brief period? The traditional consumer
analysis cannot handle this very easily observed phenomenon or,
indeed, any marked irregularity in consumption behavior of the same
type. A believer in diminishing marginal utility ought to find it even
harder to fit into his framework. In the intertemporal framework it is
easy to interpret the annual vacation as a good which gives rise to
characteristics over subsequent periods. We could elaborate on the
theme, making the annual vacation an activity that requires inputs of
goods and labor before as well as during the vacation period and gives
rise to characteristics after as well as during the period.

At the more abstract level the important consequence of goods
giving rise to characteristics in other periods is that efficiency choices
are not intertemporally independent. Thus efficiency cannot be gauged
from a single period. In particular, a good may be inefficient in giving
characteristics for period n, relative to some other good or combination
of goods, but may also give rise to some characteristics in period
$n + 1$. Taking periods n, $n + 1$ together, the good may be an efficient
choice. This relationship is independent of any properties, such as
time complementarity among characteristics, that are derived from the
utility function. Also, since efficiency depends on relative prices,
intertemporal prices become important in this case, whereas in the
completely decomposable technology only the relative prices within
each period are important.

We can also apply the intertemporal characteristics approach to
problems of durable goods depreciation. A durable good can be
regarded as a good which gives rise (alone or in conjunction with non-
durable inputs) to characteristics over general periods. The characteristics combinations may differ from period to period so that a durable
good may depreciate more rapidly in some characteristics than in
others. An automobile's reliability or performance will generally
depreciate more rapidly than its comfort or carrying capacity.

A used durable good, in terms of characteristics, can then be properly
viewed as a good with a different combination of characteristics from
that of the same good when new, rather than as simply a "shrunk"
version of a new good in traditional analysis. Once again, traditional

analysis is seen as a special case of the more general characteristics model, one in which the output of all characteristics is assumed to depreciate at the same rate.

6.5   Non-linearity and Non-additivity

In our basic model we assumed throughout that quantities of characteristics were linearly related to quantities of goods and that characteristics obtained from different goods were additive. These are simple working assumptions and also seem the most reasonable to make unless there is specific evidence to the contrary in a particular case. Nevertheless, we can expect that the assumptions are inappropriate in some cases and must be prepared to examine what happens to our analysis if we dispense with either of them.

Non-additivity presents no particular problem. If two goods, consumed together in particular proportions, give rise to a vector of characteristics which is not the sum of the vectors of characteristics of the separate goods, then we simply regard the goods combination as an activity which uses goods as inputs and produces characteristics as outputs. We then proceed with the analysis as in Section 3.9 of Chapter 3. Since we can handle activities quite generally, there is no problem with the analysis of non-additivity. The combination activity might produce characteristics vectors very different from those of the goods separately, even producing characteristics of a kind not obtainable from any of the component goods.

The possibility of non-linearity requires careful consideration. We must, at the outset, make a very clear distinction between non-linearity in the consumption technology (the quantity of a characteristic not changing in direct proportion to the change in the quantity of the good or level of the consumption activity) and diminishing psychological effects which are properties of the preference function. If the second piece of pie does not taste as good as the first, it is not because the characteristics of pie are non-linearly related to the quantity but because preference relationships are non-linear. It is of the essence of the analysis presented here that the characteristics are technically and universally related to the goods. Thus many cases of apparent non-linearity are due to inappropriate choice of characteristics—to regarding a psychological effect, instead of the objective property giving rise to it, as the characteristic. There is, however, one important class of non-linearities which are both prevalent and relate to characteristics properly defined. This is the class of discrete or integer characteristics. Some things, for example, do or do not have a certain characteristic, but it is not meaningful to speak of "more" or "less" of the characteristic.

There is always some subtlety of interpretation required in determining relevant characteristics, and many apparent integer characteristics convert directly into variations in other characteristics. A good may be made of metal or of plastic, but the relevant characteristics are the results of being made of one rather than the other—durability, for example—rather than simply being of one particular material. Obviously, an automobile is either a Plymouth Fury or it is not, but what is relevant are the characteristics which arise as a consequence of its being one particular model of automobile. There remain integer characteristics, however, which are directly relevant to choice. Some good may be available in either red or blue, and the color is relevant to choice. Since a consumer cannot trade off more or less "redness" against some other characteristic, the analysis depends on how the integer characteristic relates to preference.

Let us suppose there are three distinct goods, each available in red or blue, those being two other characteristics which are not affected by the particular color. In principle, there are six goods, G_1R, G_2R, G_3R, G_1B, G_2B, G_3B, where suffixes R, B denote red or blue. Assuming price to be independent of color, the feasible set in space of the two characteristics other than color will be of the kind drawn many times elsewhere in the book, except that each vertex will correspond to two goods, the red and blue variants, as shown in Figure 6.6. In this case any point on the frontier is attainable in either red or blue. The standard characteristics analysis holds except that each individual chooses red or blue, as he prefers. The analysis will predict the demand for each good (taking red and blue together) but not for each color of each good. This covers the most common case in which each good is available in each color.

But suppose G_2 comes only in blue, G_1, G_3 only in red. Then the situation is more complex. The consumer must then balance his color preferences against the other characteristics of the situation. We cannot draw in a third axis and treat "color" as a conventional third characteristic, since "red" and "blue" are not measurable (or even ordinally related in the objective sense) on the same axis. We can regard the efficiency frontier as being divided among two separate planes, the red

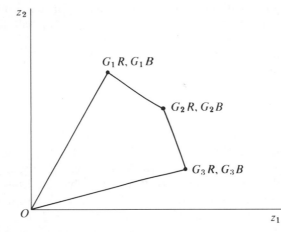

Figure 6.6. All goods available in all colors

plane and the blue plane, as shown in Figure 6.7. A particular individual will have indifference contours in the two planes, the highest contours available in the planes being denoted by I_R, I_B.

A given individual will, of course, know whether he prefers the point C in the red plane or the point D in the blue plane, but predicting market behavior from observations becomes difficult. Our consumer may prefer D (blue) to C (red), but a small increase in the price of G_3, shifting D to D', may cause him to shift to C (red). The only straightforward prediction we can expect to make is that, if the consumer is observed to prefer D to C, change in prices which does not enable him

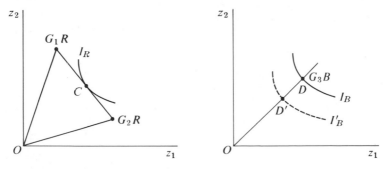

Figure 6.7. Single-color goods

to reach a higher "red" indifference curve that I_R or does not leave his attainable "blue indifference curve lower than I_B, will leave him preferring G_3 to any attainable combination of G_1 and G_2.

With discrete characteristics objective efficiency effects may still appear. To continue with the example given, a third "red" good would stand in the same relations of efficiency at various prices to other "red" goods, but efficiency relations between red and blue goods do not exist. Some discrete characteristics might be of the "zero-one" rather than "red-blue" kind. Suppose a good can be "with" or "without" something that is universally considered desirable but is not quantitative, and possesses two other quantitative characteristics. We can then predict that any combination of the basic characteristics z_1 and z_2 "with" will be universally preferred to the same combination of z_1 and z_2 "without." This gives us more predictive power than in the "red-blue" case, but we still cannot predict whether a "with" combination of z_1 and z_2 will or will not be universally preferred to a "without" combination having a shade more of both z_1 and z_2.

Part II

TOWARD APPLICATION

CHAPTER 7

MAKING THE THEORY OPERATIONAL

7.1 Bridging the Gap

The characteristics analysis of demand behavior has great operational potential. Characteristics are taken to be objective properties of goods (or consumption activities), and the model implies predictions— efficiency effects—of a universal nature, not dependent on individual preferences. Furthermore, predictions of the demand for new goods and new product differentiates are implied.

Operational use of the model requires identification of the relevant characteristics and data on the consumption technology. Neither of these requirements is yet easily met, partly because of the conceptual problems of identifying relevant characteristics and partly because the appropriate data have not hitherto been available. The data problem is of the kind that arises commonly with new ways of looking at things. Data collection commences only when a potential use for the data is provided. Some data of the appropriate kind do exist, however, and many could be collected in principle.

The author believes it is the task of the theorist to provide the basic guidelines along which more empirical research may be conducted. Economic models are ill served by a precipitous rush (especially by thesis-hungry graduate students) to "measure" or "test" the models in a crude formulation and with inappropriate data. To the extent that the model builder fails to provide operational guidance, he has only himself to blame if empirical work, purportedly related to the original model, dissolves into a set of regression equations in which the original model is unrecognizable, or in which the discrimination between his and a dozen other models has been lost in simplification or linearization.

The purpose of this and the succeeding chapters is to travel some of the distance between the basic abstract model and direct operational use of the model. We shall not travel the whole distance but terminate it at the point where the principles for empirical investigation and application have been established—at the point where, if all requisite data fell at our feet, we could pick them up and use them appropriately.

7.2   Operational Definition of a Characteristic

The key to operational use of the model lies in taking the proper view of what constitutes a characteristic in the sense of the analysis. It is essential that the characteristic be an objective, universal property of the good (or activity). The spirit of the whole analysis requires that personal reactions are reactions to the characteristic, not reactions about what the characteristic is. Thus the calorie content of a food or the cooling power of an air-conditioner is a characteristic—it is an objective property—but "beauty," which is presumably in the eye of the beholder, is not. If an object is thought to be beautiful by some it is because of some objective characteristic(s) such as shape or color pattern. The shape may be characteristic (or rather a complex of characteristics), the beauty is a reaction to the shape. Since aesthetic reactions are usually reactions to an extremely complex mix of a very large number of characteristics, we shall not pretend that our model will be operationally useful when aesthetic considerations are dominant in choice. The day may come when a computer can analyze the difference between an acclaimed work of literature and a piece of doggerel in terms of the objective arrangement of words, but it has not yet arrived.

Thus we commence our search for characteristics of a good from the good itself, not from people's reactions to it. Every objective property of size, shape, performance is a potential characteristic. In principle, if we take an object, measure it in every possible dimension and in every aspect of performance, in every biological, chemical, and physical aspect, we have evaluated all its possible characteristics. When this is said, it becomes immediately obvious that the operational problems concerning the use of the characteristics analysis do not lie in the measuring of the characteristics (since they are objective, this is simply a technical matter) but in selecting which characteristics to measure. Even the simplest of things possesses a myriad of objective properties. We could take, for example, an orange: measure its diameter, weight, skin thickness, ratio of juice weight to solid matter, sugar content, vitamin C content, wavelength of light reflected from it (color). All these properties might be relevant to consumer choice. But we could also measure it elasticity, moment of inertia, air resistance, exact center of gravity—surely not relevant to choice of an orange, but highly relevant to the choice of a baseball.

Our fundamental operational problem is determining the relevant characteristics for choice. Once we have listed those characteristics which are actually relevant, we can proceed to take the appropriate measurements. In other words, if we were to discover that dietetic properties represented the only relevant characteristics for consumer choice among foods (highly improbable), we would accept the biochemist's measures of the diet contents. In some instances the economist might end up measuring characteristics himself, simply because no one else had done it, but he would not be acting in his role as economist while so doing.

Note that this approach to measurement runs against the current tradition in economics. What we are advocating is that, once relevant characteristics have been identified, we give the problem of measurement of the technical goods-characteristics relationships over to physical scientists and engineers rather than to econometricians. This does not mean, of course, that econometrics is not involved in the total problem. In this model there are two distinct relationships involved, the technical goods-characteristics relationships and the people-characteristics relationships. The first can be determined—in a forward direction, so to speak—by engineers, whereas the second can only be estimated back from observed market behavior, in the tradition of econometrics.

7.3   The Problems of Operationalization

Our model or demand behavior is, as has been stressed earlier, a "fine structure" model, designed to explain market behavior with respect to goods defined in a very narrow sense—each product is differentiated as a different good. This means that we are concerned with the spectrum of varieties or models within a broadly defined market, not with such aggregates as "food" or "automobiles." For such composite commodities the simpler and cruder traditional analysis is appropriate. At the same time the consumer is facing a consumption technology in which any specific characteristic might be obtained from any good. Thus the consumer's universe is, in principle, the complete set of all possible varieties of all possible goods—an astronomical number of goods, and presumably of characteristics.

The first requirement for any attempt at operational use of the model, therefore, is to find the circumstances (assuming they exist) under which we can analyze part of the total consumption universe in relative isolation from the remainder. We seek conditions under which the analysis of goods can be carried out in groups, one group at a time. This problem is discussed in Chapter 8. If no justification could be found for considering, say, automobiles as a group and analyzing the automobile market by itself, then the model would be too large and complex to be useful. We anticipate finding that group analysis can be carried out (after all, consumers themselves must subdivide their universe), although the investigation is not by any means trivial. The separable group, it should be noted, need not coincide with the set of goods commonly regarded as forming a given "market," although we can expect that it will frequently so coincide.

Once we have established the possibility of concentrating on a group of goods of manageable size, the chief operational problems are those of identifying the characteristics relevant to this particular group. When the characteristics are properly identified, the problems of finding the consumption subtechnology are practical rather than conceptual, as shown in the previous section.

Chapters 9 and 10 are concerned with criteria by which we can decide whether to discard some objective property as an irrelevant characteristic from the viewpoint of market analysis, or by which we can decide that we have not included all relevant characteristics in our analysis. Before turning to investigate these problems in detail, we shall relax and dream a little. Assuming the problems to be solved, we can look at some potential recipes for using our operationalized theory.

7.4   Untried Recipe 1: Estimating the Demand for a New Good

As an illustration of the operational possibilities of the model set out in this book let us consider the problem of estimating the demand for a new good. Solution of this problem is not conceptually possible with traditional demand theory, and attempts to solve it have been in terms of an implicit characteristics approach, considering the new good to be "like" some existing good, for example.

A sophisticated attempt to solve this kind of problem for new types of transport (including some not yet made practical) was made by Baumol and Quandt,[1] using an approach very similar in spirit to that set out here. They attempted to estimate the demand for each aspect or "abstract mode" of transportation (speed, etc.), then to estimate the demand for new types of travel by treating each type as a combination of the various modes. The abstract mode is, in principle, a characteristic in our sense. However, the method of estimating shadow prices for the abstract modes is different from that implied by the full characteristics model.

Let us suppose we have a new good, never before sold on the market. We have data on all its characteristics, and we take it that the consumption technology permits analysis of goods in groups. We wish to estimate the potential market demand for the good, in the economist's sense of a demand schedule showing quantities that would be purchased at various prices for a specified income distribution and for given prices of other goods. In principle the problem can be solved completely in terms of the characteristics model provided the relevant characteristics possessed by the new good are possessed (but in different proportions and combinations) by existing goods. If the major characteristic or characteristics are not related to characteristics of existing goods, we can do no better (but no worse) than in the traditional analysis.

We assume:

(1) That the new good fits into some group of goods, defined by a manageable number of relevant characteristics which can be treated in isolation from the rest of the consumption economy. This is not strictly necessary for solution of the problem, but it is required for a manageable solution:

(2) That data on the characteristics of all other goods in the group are available.

(3) That market data for the existing group (without the new good) are available.

(4) That the consumption subtechnology for the group is linear and additive.

[1] R. E. Quandt and W. J. Baumol, "The demand for abstract transport modes: theory and measurement," *Journal of Regional Sciences*, Vol. 6, 1966, pp. 13–26.

The demand for the new good will depend on where it fits into the efficiency frontier for this group of goods and on the distribution of preferences and incomes (for a group, on the distribution of budgets for group goods rather than total incomes). The existing efficiency frontier can be constructed directly from the technical data on characteristics and the prices of goods already on the market, in the manner discussed at length in Chapter 4. Let us suppose, for illustration, that our group contains three goods (excluding the new good), that there

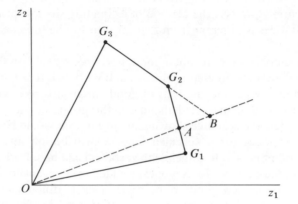

Figure 7.1. Existing efficiency frontier

are only two relevant characteristics in the group, and that the consumption technology and prices are those used several times in earlier illustrations, namely

$$B = \begin{bmatrix} 2 & 1.8 & 1 \\ 1 & 1.8 & 2 \end{bmatrix}$$
$$p = \begin{bmatrix} 1 & 1 & 1 \end{bmatrix}$$

Figure 7.1 [identical with Figures 3.1(b) and 5.2] shows the existing efficiency frontier.

Now suppose the new good G_N possesses characteristics z_1, z_2 in proportions $3:2$. The point in C-space corresponding to the new good will be along the broken ray in the diagram, between goods G_1 and G_2. The maximum price at which the new good could be sold at all (assuming prices of G_1, G_2, G_3 are constant at unity) would be that which puts it just on the existing efficiency frontier, at point A in the diagram. This can be computed without market information, since it depends on efficiency relationships only. If one unit of G_N contains 3 units of z_1 and 2 of z_2, it is easily calculated that the maximum salable price is 1.556.

We cannot proceed further and project demand without some knowledge of *preference distribution*. This must be estimated from market data. Note that, as was shown in Chapter 4, the only potential customers for the new good at prices close to, but below, 1.556 will be those consumers choosing points on the facet G_1G_2 under existing market conditions. Consumers choosing points on the facet G_2G_3 will have no interest in the new good unless its price is sufficiently low for G_2 to be dominated by it—corresponding to a point further out than B in the figure. Market data will not show the distribution of consumption along the facet but will show only the quantities of the goods actually purchased. The distribution of preferences, or strictly speaking, of "market weights" (see Chapter 5), must be estimated from the data on sales.

This estimation, unlike the technical measurement of characteristics, involves all the art and science of econometrics. A given hypothesis concerning preference and income distribution (combined in market weights) will predict the sales of the various goods. Working backward, therefore, we shall select a suitable functional form for the distribution and determine its parameters by fitting to the data on sales. Let us suppose that the market data show sales of 100 for G_1 and 400 for G_2 and that all data and hypothesis are exact, with no stochastic problems. Let us also make the hypothesis that the distribution over the range to which facet G_1G_2 is relevant is: (i) independent of the distribution among consumers whose preferences lead them to choose on facet G_2G_3; (ii) determined by the distribution of the parameter α in Cobb-Douglas preference functions $U(\alpha) = z_1^{\alpha} z_1^{1-\alpha}$, in which (iii) the distribution of α is given by the linearly skewed distribution function $f(\alpha) = A + 2B\alpha$, where A, B are the parameters to be determined.

The distribution function here is equivalent to having two populations, one of size A having rectangularly distributed preferences, the over of size B with a simple skewed distribution, and with total sales the sum of sales to the two populations. In Chapter 5 (Section 5.8) it was shown that, for precisely the efficiency frontier of our current problem, sales of G_1 and G_2 to the two populations would be:

	Rectangular Distribution $f^1(\alpha) = A$	Skewed Distribution $f^2(\alpha) = 2B\alpha$
Good 1	0.155A	0.291B
Good 2	0.69A	0.683B

We, therefore, determine A, B from the equations

$$0.155A + 0.291B = 100$$
$$0.69A \ \ + 0.683B = 400$$

which give, approximately

$$A = 492$$
$$B = 89$$

Thus the distribution of market weights is given by

$$f(\alpha) = 492 + 178\alpha$$

Having estimated the distribution, we can then use it to predict the demand for the new good, on the assumption that the estimated distribution can be presumed to hold for the slightly different real income levels that will result when the existing efficiency frontier is changed. Figure 7.2 shows the efficiency frontier after the introduction of the new good (G_N) at a price somewhat lower than the maximum salable level. Given the distribution of market weights, we calculate the distribution of facet consumers along G_2G_N and G_1G_N, and of vertex consumers on G_1, G_N, G_2, just as we did for the numerical examples of Chapter 5. The sales of goods G_1, G_2, G_N are then computed, giving the demand for G_N at the price assumed and, incidentally, showing the effect of G_N on the sales of G_1 and G_2.

In making these calculations we determine the new geometry of the efficiency frontier in terms of the particular price of the new good for which demand is to be calculated. This gives the slopes of the facets. We then calculate separately the demand from the rectangularly distributed portion of the market and the skewed portion, adding the two. Since the arithmetic is tedious, results are not given even for the numerical example we have been using, but the calculations are straightforward enough. Similar calculations can be made for alternative prices of the new good, building up the demand properties. How great a price range for which we choose to do this depends primarily on the extent to which we are willing to assume that the estimated distribution holds when we move a considerable distance beyond the original efficiency frontier.

In practice, of course, estimation of the distribution of market weights will involve stochastic assumptions and much ingenuity. If we were to fit a two-parameter distribution to data for sales of all three

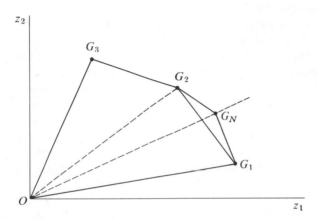

Figure 7.2. Introduction of new good

goods in the above example, we sould need to specify where the random variable fitted into the system. We might assume that consumers make random errors in assessing the technical goods-characteristics relationships, that the preference distribution was subject to a random element, or that the quantities sold were subject to a stochastic element. It is clearly premature to worry about the stochastic properties of the system at this stage.

7.5   Untried Recipe 2: Constant-Characteristic Economic Evaluations

Since automobiles did not exist in the nineteenth century, and horse carriages are not used in the twentieth, a clear problem arises in many types of economic evaluation concerning transport in the two centuries. The relative costs of private transport cannot be adequately represented by traditional price indexes, for example, when the goods are quite different in the two periods, although various indirect methods can be used, such as chaining over a period when both forms of transport were in existence. This is simply and extreme case, however, since models and varieties of goods change over relatively short periods, giving rise to precisely the same comparability problem in principle. The use of the characteristics approach would seem to provide some possibility of making comparisons of this kind. Automobiles surely possess some characteristics which were also shared by carriages, and most model and variety changes involve changes in proportions of characteristics rather than the introduction of entirely new characteristics.

A related problem is that of quality changes. New models are introduced, prices change. Has the price of the good, per unit of "quality," changed or not? Again, the idea of quality is a broad generalization of the idea of characteristic content. "Quality improvement" means, if anything, increased quantities of some characteristics per unit of the good, and some kind of approach via the characteristics analysis seems mandatory. Some of the work in this area, especially that of Griliches,[2] represents an early attempt to solve the problem in this way.

A deeper set of problems, but of a related kind, concern the evaluations of the consumer technology as a whole. Does the modern urban dweller really obtain as much more of relevant characteristics, compared with the simple peasant, as suggested by standard comparisons of GNP per head? Clearly, some characteristics (freedom from noise and some kinds of pollutions) are provided free in certain consumer technologies but must be purchased (via goods or activities) at some cost in other technologies.

We can attempt answers to these problems much better by looking at characteristics than at goods themselves. How much does it cost, in different periods or different countries, to obtain some fixed bundle of characteristics by the most efficient choice of goods for the purpose? Surely this is a much better index of comparison for welfare and other evaluative purposes than the price of a fixed bundle of goods.

There are two major advantages to economic evaluation in terms of characteristics rather than goods. One is the straightforward advantage of being able to sail through the otherwise dangerous problems concerning new goods, model changes, and so on. The other, which

[2] Z. Griliches, "Hedonic price indexes for automobiles," in National Bureau of Economic Research, *Price Statistics of the Federal Government*, 1961.

may be much more important, is the ability to take the characteristics collection as a whole and thus take account of such things as negative effects and interactions. With the characteristics approach we can attempt to solve some of the old problems about which things are costs and which are benefits, always hidden in the goods evaluation approach. If supersonic aircraft are so noisy that everyone must wear earmuffs, the traditional goods-counting approach (as in using GNP as an evaluative index) will count the production and purchase of earmuffs an addition to the good things of life. The total characteristics approach will correctly note that the earmuffs merely cancel negative amounts of characteristics from other goods and bring no net benefit.

A constant-characteristics evaluation index will typically involve changes in the collection of goods used to attain the chosen bundle of characteristics. If the goods collection is constant, the characteristics approach has no superiority over the traditional goods indices. The technique for constructing a constant-characteristics index is solving, at each time or place of evaluation, for the *most efficient* use of goods to achieve those characteristics. Stigler's original diet problem[3] is the prototype of such a construction, although realistic indices must take account of sufficient characteristics to cover those relevant to choice. Thus the construction of the index is not merely a question of inserting prices or quantities into a fixed weighting problem but of computing appropriate weights (typically a program in linear programming) at each point.

Suppose, to take our simple numerical example again, we have a 2-characteristic, 3-good universe with technology

$$B = \begin{bmatrix} 2 & 1.8 & 1 \\ 1 & 1.8 & 2 \end{bmatrix}$$

Prices p_1, p_3 of G_1, G_3 are constant at 1, while p_2 takes on successive values 1, 1.2, 1.4. The efficiency frontiers are shown in Figure 7.3(a), (b), (c).

We seek to construct a constant-characteristic price index, the base bundle of characteristics being [1, 1]. At $p_2 = 1$, the most efficient method of attaining the base collection is by purchase of G_2 only. The quantity of G_2 required to attain the characteristics collection is 0.56, costing 0.56 at unit price. At $p_2 = 1.2$, it is equally efficient to attain

[3] G. J. Stigler, "The cost of subsistence," *Journal of Farm Economics*, Vol. XXVII, 1945.

the base characteristics collection by (a) purchasing 0.56 unit of G_2 or
(b) purchasing 0.33 unit of G_1 and 0.33 unit of G_3. In either case, the
cost of the base collection is 0.67. Note that, for values of p_2 less than
1.2, the constant-characteristics index depends only on p_2. A traditional
goods-index, taking prices of all three goods into account, would be
equivalent to choosing an inefficient point somewhere in the triangle

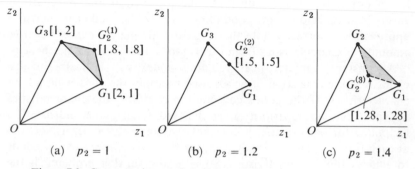

Figure 7.3. Constant-characteristic index numbers

$G_1G_2G_3$ and would thus overstate the cost of attaining the characteristic
collection.

For $p_2 > 1.2$, G_2 is no longer an efficient choice. At $p_2 = 1.4$, the
efficient choice is 0.33 unit of G_1 and 0.33 unit of G_3, for a cost of 0.67.
It is the prices of G_1, G_3 which now determine the value of the index,
not the price of G_2. In our simple example, G_2 should disappear from
the market at $p_2 > 1.2$, but, in practice, we might expect some sales of
G_2 still to take place. A traditional fixed-weight goods index would
represent an inefficient point and again overstate the costs.

CHAPTER 8

GROUP ANALYSIS

8.1 Reducing the Universe

The consumption technology is, in principle, a statement of the whole consumers' world, that is, of the relationship between all goods available in the economy and all characteristics to which any consumer has any reaction. The most basic problem of producing any operational versions of the model is to reduce the scope of a particular aspect of consumer behavior to smaller dimensions, to something less than the consumers' total world.

In traditional theory the most usual reduction of scope of a world of n goods is to that of a notional two-good analysis in which one of the goods is a clearly defined single good and the other is a conceptional "composite good." The warrant for this reduction is the *composite good theorem*, first proved by Hicks.[1] This theorem enables us to treat a composite commodity, defined as an index number formed from $n - 1$ of the goods, as if it were a single good, provided the relative prices of the $n - 1$ goods do not change. We then use a two-good analysis with the real good and the composite. This analysis is simple and can be used to discuss the general properties of the demand for a single good, when the prices of all other goods remain fixed.

In principle the same technique can be used to investigate the relationships between some groups of k goods, reducing the problem to $k + 1$ dimensions by replacing the remaining $n - k$ goods with a

[1] J. R. Hicks, *Value and Capital* (2nd Ed.), Oxford, 1946.

composite good. Nevertheless, groups of goods present a major problem in the traditional model because there is no structure provided for singling out one set of goods as belonging to a "group" in the sense that they have more in common with each other than with goods not in the group. In the traditional model the only source of structure is the structure of preferences, and we have neither theory nor empirical evidence relating to this.

For practical purposes grouping of goods is needed even with traditional theory. Such grouping is usually made on the basis of the intrinsic properties of goods even though the theory, in principle, has no place for grouping on this basis. Thus we might consider such groups as "men's clothing," "automobiles," "vegetables" and consider consumer behavior within the group even though the theory as such gives no reason to suppose that a consumer's choice concerning lamb chops is more closely related to this choice concerning steak than to his choice concerning shirts. In fact, by grouping goods, we have all made implicit use of the characteristics of goods for years. We can formally and explicitly incorporate our previously implicit and theoretically unwarranted technique of grouping goods by doing this in terms of the structure of the consumption technology.

8.2   Intrinsic Groups

If we can assume an essentially linear consumption technology, we can search for "natural" or "intrinsic" groups in terms of the structure of technology matrix itself. Such groups, being defined on the structure of the consumption technology rather than on the structure of preferences, will be universal.

The most obvious structure that would seem to provide a clearly defined intrinsic group is one which is completely separable. Such a the technology would be one in which there was a subset of goods and a subset of characteristics such that (i) no good in the goods subset possessed any characteristic not in the characteristics subset; (ii) no characteristic in the characteristics subset was possessed by any good not in the goods subset. With complete separability of this kind, the technology matrix can always be permuted so that it can be partitioned into four submatrices, two of which are zero matrices as shown below:

$$\begin{bmatrix} B_1 & 0 \\ 0 & B_2 \end{bmatrix}$$

The submatrix B_1 can be of any order. If there are n goods and r characteristics and B_1 is of order $s \times k$, then B_2 will be of order $(r - s) \times (n - k)$ and the upper and lower zero matrices of order $s \times (n - k)$ and $(r - s) \times k$, respectively. We shall consider B_1 to represent the subtechnology of the particular group in which we are interested, which contains k goods and possesses s characteristics. B_2, representing the rest of the technology, might be further separable to give any number of groups. A good in the subset represented in B_1 can be referred to as technically unrelated to any good not in the subset.

Since efficiency substitution effects arise only when a particular characteristics vector can be attained efficiently by a change in the goods vector as a result of changes in the relative price of goods, we can immediately state the following:

There are no efficiency substitution effects between technically unrelated goods. With a completely separable technology, efficiency substitution effects are confined within each goods group.

This does not mean, of course, that there are no substitution effects between technically unrelated goods. Insofar as there is substitution between characteristics (the personal substitution effect), there will be indirect substitution even between goods which are technically unrelated.

If characteristics have been correctly chosen we may well expect that the substitutability between the characteristics of different separable groups is lower than between the characteristics within each group. This would give higher personal substitution effects within a group than between groups. Coupled with efficiency substitution effects, which occur only within groups, this gives the usual expectation that substitution within groups will be greater than between technically unrelated goods.

It is possible, however, that this is not the case. An individual may have lower substitutability between characteristics within a group than between characteristics of different groups, and the efficiency substitution effects may not be sufficient to overcome this difference. Thus we might have larger overall substitution effects between technically unrelated goods than within a group. An intrinsic grouping based on the structure of the technology might, therefore, fail to coincide with an empirically determined grouping based on cross elasticities.

We shall generally assume in our analysis that private substitution effects are greater within a group than across groups and, given the additional efficiency substitution effects, that the overall substitution effects are noticeably higher within groups than across groups.

The condition for valid demand analysis of goods within an intrinsic group, treating the group as if it were the whole relevant universe of the consumer, do not depend on the relative strengths of substitution effects within the group and across groups, but on other properties of the preference functions. We shall discuss these in Section 8.3.

8.3   Isolated Analysis of the Group

The most useful situation for operational employment of the group concept is one in which (i) the group is intrinsic and defined by a completely separable technology; (ii) the group can be analyzed in isolation.

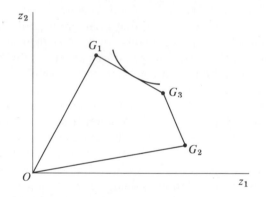

Figure 8.1. Three-good, two-characteristic technology

That is, on the assumption that prices or other relevant parameters for goods outside the group remain constant, we can look at the group as though the set of characteristics associated with it are the only relevant characteristics for the time being.

Consider Figure 8.1, which is simply a repetition of the standard illustration for the three-good two-characteristic technology. In previous analysis this was taken to represent the consumers' universe. We now seek to establish the conditions under which we can treat such a diagram, drawn for a group of three goods, in exactly the same way that we did when it represented the whole universe of goods and characteristics. Suppose that the universe consists of one other characteristic, z_3, and one other good G_4, in addition to the group of goods G_1–G_3 and the characteristics z_1 and z_2. Characteristic z_3 is not possessed by any of the goods in the group.

Since the basic demand analysis is case in terms of the general shapes of the efficiency frontier and indifference curves, it is sufficient to be able to analyze the group in a similar way so that these shapes are independent of the quantity of good G_4. That is, variations in the quantity of G_4 should play the same role as an income effect alone in the universal analysis.

For a regular budget constraint on the four goods the feasible set in C-space will be three dimensional. But consider the boundary contour of the feasible set of $z_3 = \bar{z}_3$. Since z_3 is obtained only from G_4, some specific amount $\bar{x}_4$ of G_4 is required to attain quantity $\bar{z}_3$ of characteristic z_3. If the price of G_4 is p_4, and k is the total budget, the amount remaining to be spent on goods in the group is $k - p_4\bar{x}_4$.

Provided that G_4 possesses nothing of characteristics z_1 and z_2, combinations of these characteristics can be obtained only from combinations of G_1, G_2, and G_3. Thus the feasible set in C'-space (the space of the characteristics pertaining to the group) will be exactly the same as it would be in C-space of (i) were z_1 and z_2 the only characteristics and G_1, G_2, and G_3 the only goods, and if (ii) the budget were $k - p_4\bar{x}_4$. Thus the feasible set in C'-space has a shape which depends only on the goods-characteristics coefficients and prices of goods within the group, and all effects due to G_4 appear as pure scale changes in the feasible set for the group.

The above case can be illustrated geometrically, as in Figure 8.2. This figure shows the complete feasible set, with extreme points O, G_1, G_2, G_3, G_4. For any given quantity of characteristic $\bar{z}_3$, the available choices for z_1 and z_2 are given by the intersection of a horizontal plane, height $\bar{z}_3$ above the z_1z_2 plane, with the complete feasible set. Such an intersection, illustrated by $O'G'G_2'G_3'$ in the diagram, is clearly of exactly the same shape as the intersection $OG_1G_2G_3$ of the feasible set and the z_1z_2 plane but is reduced in a scalar fashion. To treat goods G_1, G_2, G_3 as a group is equivalent to taking $OG_1G_2G_3$ as the relevant feasible set. This differs from the true feasible set, for each $\bar{z}_3$, only by a scalar multiple.

We can generalize easily to cases in which there are many characteristics and many goods outside the group, provided the goods in the group possess none of these characteristics and the goods outside the group possesses none of the group characteristics.

A sufficient condition for the feasible set in C'-space (group characteristics space) to be subject only to pure scale changes as a result of events outside the group is that the group be intrinsic and defined by a completely separable consumption technology.

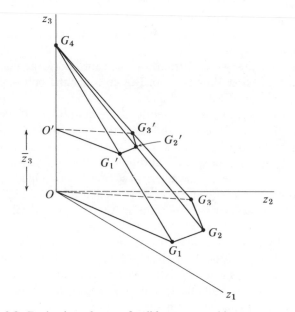

Figure 8.2. Derivation of group feasible set, separable case

The conditions to be satisfied for preferences are rather more complex. For the "shape" of the indifference contours in C'-space to the unaffected by the quantity of goods outside the group (hence characteristics outside the group), it is necessary that the direction of the normal to the tangent plane at any point on the contour be unaffected by the quantities of characteristics outside the group. For the four-good, three-characteristic universe in which G_1, G_2, G_3, and z_1, z_2 form a group, the condition requires that the slope of an indifference curve in C'-space be independent of z_3. If preferences are indexed by a function $U(z_1, z_2, z_3)$, this condition can be written

$$\frac{\partial}{\partial z_3}\left(\frac{u_1}{u_2}\right) = 0$$

This condition is satisfied by the Cobb-Douglas type of function. If

$$u(z_1, z_2, z_3) = z_1{}^\alpha z_2{}^\beta z_3{}^\gamma$$

then

$$\frac{u_1}{u_2} = \frac{\alpha}{\beta}\frac{z_2}{z_1}$$

and

$$\frac{\partial}{\partial z_3}\left(\frac{u_1}{u_2}\right) = 0$$

More generally, if the set of indices of characteristics within the group is denoted by G, the condition becomes

$$\frac{\partial}{\partial z_k}\left(\frac{u_i}{u_j}\right) = 0 \quad \text{for all } i, j \in G, k \notin G$$

This is clearly satisfied by a generalized Cobb-Douglas form

$$u(z_1, \ldots, z_r) = z_1{}^{\alpha_1} z_2{}^{\alpha_2} \cdots z_r{}^{\alpha_r}$$

The Cobb-Douglas form oversatisfies the condition since it is true for all i, j, k (provided $k \neq i$ or j) in this case. If we order the characteristics so that the first s is relevant to the group, the condition is satisfied by any function that is multiplicatively separable (or logarithmically additive) in the following way:

$$u(z_1 \cdots z_r) = \phi(z_1 \cdots z_s) \cdot \psi(z_{s+1} \cdots z_r)$$

In this case we have

$$u_i = \Psi \cdot \phi_i \qquad (i \leqq s)$$

so that

$$\frac{u_i}{u_j} = \frac{\phi_i}{\phi_j} \qquad (i, j \leqq s)$$

and

$$\frac{\partial}{\partial z_k}\left(\frac{u_i}{u_j}\right) = 0 \quad (k > s, i, j \leqq s)$$

We can now state:

A sufficient condition for the shapes of indifference contours in C'-space (group characteristics space) to be unaffected by events outside the group is that the preference (utility) function can be expressed as the product of two functions, one of characteristics in the group only, the other of characteristics outside the group only.

The Cobb-Douglas form is simply a special case of a multiplicatively separable function. Since we have found the Cobb-Douglas form useful for simple models of preference distribution, and since it satisfies the condition for group isolation, we can assert:

The simple model of demand behavior, based on a linear technology and distributed Cobb-Douglas preferences, can be applied without modification to demand within a group, provided the group is defined by a completely separable technology matrix.

8.4   Universal Characteristics

Complete separability of the technology matrix provides the ideal case for use of analysis by groups, but it is a very stringent condition on the structure of the technology. It is clearly desirable to discuss the possibilities of preserving group analysis under somewhat weakened conditions.

If we consider possible ways in which a real group might satisfy some, but not all, of the separability conditions, one of the cases of great practical importance would seem to be that of a group with the following structural relations. The group consists of a subset of goods which possess characteristics that can be divided into two subsets: (1) a subset of characteristics possessed by no goods outside the group; (2) a subset of characteristics which are also processed by all, or a large number of, other goods in the universe. We shall refer to the characteristics of the second subset as *universal characteristics*. The characteristics of the first subset can be unambiguously referred to as *group characteristics*.

The technology matrix below illustrates a structure of this kind for two groups each of three-good and two-group characteristics, with a single universal characteristic. A seventh good which possesses the universal characteristic only (and cannot therefore be considered as a single-good group) is also included. Stars in the matrix refer to elements that are typically non-zero, although some may be zero.

	Group I goods			Group II goods			
Group I characteristics	*	*	*	0	0	0	0
	*	*	*	0	0	0	0
Group II characteristics	0	0	0	*	*	*	0
	0	0	0	*	*	*	0
Universal characteristic	*	*	*	*	*	*	*

We shall approach the analysis of the universal characteristics problem by considering a very simple technology of three characteristics and four goods. The first three goods form a group, with the first two characteristics as their group characteristics. The third characteristic is a universal characteristic, and it is the only characteristic possessed by the fourth good.
The technology matrix is:

$$
\begin{array}{l}
\text{Group characteristics} \\
\\
\text{Universal characteristic}
\end{array}
\begin{bmatrix}
b_{11} & b_{12} & b_{13} & 0 \\
b_{21} & b_{22} & b_{23} & 0 \\
b_{31} & b_{32} & b_{33} & b_{34}
\end{bmatrix}
$$

For a regular budget constraint $p_1 x_1 + p_2 x_2 + p_3 x_3 + p_4 x_4 = k$, we obtain a feasible set in C-space (the space of all three characteristics) of the kind illustrated in Figure 8.3. We are interested in the feasible set in C'-space (the space of the two-group characteristics) for different values of z_3, that is, in the contours of the feasible set for $z_3 = \bar{z}_3$. One such contour is shown in Figure 8.3.

In the completely separable case non-group characteristics were obtainable only from non-group goods so that setting a level for these characteristics merely determined expenditures on non-group goods and thus the budget available for the group. Here the situation is more complicated, since part of the universal characteristic will be obtained from group goods.

Consider specifically the quantity of good 1 that can be obtained by spending the whole budget only on goods 1 and 4, subject to the quantity $\bar{z}_3$ of the universal characteristic being obtained. We have two constraints:

$$p_1 x_1 + p_4 x_4 = k$$
$$b_{31} x_1 + b_{34} x_4 = \bar{z}_3$$

The two equations give a unique solution provided the matrix

$$\begin{bmatrix} p_1 & p_4 \\ b_{31} & b_{34} \end{bmatrix}$$

is non-singular. Singularity here would imply $p_1/b_{31} = p_4/b_{34}$, that is,

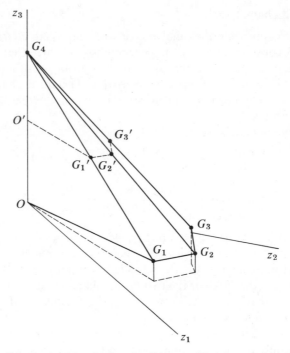

Figure 8.3. Derivation of group feasible set with universal characteristic

the cost of obtaining a unit of the universal characteristic was the same
whether it was obtained by buying G_1 or G_4. Since this would require G_4
to be inefficient (since the universal characteristic is its only characteristic, while G_1 provides other characteristics as well), we can rule it
out. Indeed, if G_4 is to be efficient, the cost per unit of universal

characteristic must be *less* through G_4 than through G_1, that is,

$$\frac{p_1}{b_{31}} > \frac{p_4}{b_{34}}$$

which makes the determinant

$$D = \begin{vmatrix} p_1 & p_4 \\ b_{31} & b_{34} \end{vmatrix}$$

positive.

But we have an implicit non-negativity condition to be considered. We must have $x_1, x_4 \geqq 0$. If we solve the two constraint equations by the usual Cramer's method, the values for x_1, x_4 are the ratio of two determinants D_1 and D_4 to D, where

$$D_1 = \begin{vmatrix} k & p_4 \\ \bar{z}_3 & b_{34} \end{vmatrix} \qquad D_4 = \begin{vmatrix} p_1 & k \\ b_{31} & \bar{z}_3 \end{vmatrix}$$

Since we have taken D to be essentially positive, D_1 and D_4 must be non-negative. The conditions for D_1 and D_4 to be non-negative can be written as

$$\frac{k}{p_4} \geqq \frac{\bar{z}_3}{b_{34}}$$

$$\frac{\bar{z}_3}{b_{31}} \geqq \frac{k}{p_4}$$

k/p_4 is the maximum amount of G_4 that can be purchased with the budget, and $\bar{z}_3/b_{34}$ is the amount of G_4 necessary to provide the stated quantity of the universal characteristic from G_4 alone. Corresponding interpretations can be attached to the ratios for G_1. Similar conditions can be derived for the relationship between x_2, x_4 and x_3, x_4.

Combining these conditions with that found earlier for D to be positive, we can give the general restriction on the technology, prices, budget, and amount of universal characteristic necessary to give valid results:

(1) The cost of obtaining a unit of universal characteristic should be less through purchase of the good possessing only that characteristic than through the purchase of a group good.

(2) The required quantity of universal characteristic could be obtained by expenditure on goods entirely outside the group.

(3) The required quantity of universal characteristic could not be (or could only just be) obtained by expenditure entirely within the group.

These conditions are not unduly restrictive, since they will be satisfied easily when the group goods possess the universal characteristic only to a minor degree, but a major amount of this characteristic is required from the complete goods collection. Assuming those conditions to be satisfied, we return to the problem of determining the feasible set in group-characteristics space.

For the given quantity of $\bar{z}_3$, the maximum amount of G_1 that can be purchased with the budget is then given by

$$x_1 = \frac{D_1}{D}$$

$$= \frac{k - p_4 \dfrac{z_3}{b_{34}}}{p_1 - p_4 \dfrac{b_{31}}{b_{34}}}$$

with equivalent results for x_2, x_3.

The numerator of the above fraction has the dimension of a budget. It is, in fact, the total budget less the expenditure necessary to obtain the required amount of z_3 by purchasing G_4 only. The denominator has the dimensions of price. It is the price of G_1 adjusted by subtraction of the term $p_4 b_{31}/b_{34}$. This term represents the cost of obtaining the amount of universal characteristic embodied in one unit of G_1 by purchasing G_4 rather than G_1. Since an equivalent relationship holds for x_2, x_3 the "adjusted budget" (the numerator in the expression given for x_1) is the same for x_1, x_2, and x_3.

If there is a universal characteristic, the feasible set in C'-space is found by proceeding as though the group goods and group characteristics comprised the relevant universe except that (i) the adjusted budget constraint is used with the adjusted budget equal to the total budget less the expenditure necessary to obtain the required amount of the universal characteristic from goods outside the group; (ii) the prices to be assigned to the group goods are not the market prices but adjusted prices obtained by subtracting from the market price of each good, the cost of obtaining the amount of universal characteristic embodied in a unit of that good from outside the group.

The adjusted budget is completely independent of the prices, technology, or quantities of the group goods. It depends only on the overall budget constraint, the stated requirement of universal characteristic, and the technical properties of goods outside the group. The adjusted prices represent distortions of the ordinary market prices for goods within the group and also depend on the prices of non-group goods so that we cannot proceed as though the shape of the feasible set is invariant to events outside the group.

Expressed as a proportion, the distortion of market prices to obtain adjusted prices (that is, the percentage by which market prices must be reduced) is given by

$$\frac{p_4}{p_i} \cdot \frac{b_{3i}}{b_{34}}$$

for the ith good in the group. This represents the ratio of the cost of obtaining a unit of the universal characteristic from outside the group to that of obtaining a unit of universal characteristic from the ith good itself.

If the ratio is the same for all goods within the group, all the adjusted prices will bear the same ratio to market prices, and the shape of the feasible set will be the same as the shape when market prices are used.

The individual ratios depend on p_4, but the condition that they be equal does not. The distortion ratio will be the same for all goods in the group if

$$p_i/b_{3i} = p_j/b_{3j} \qquad \text{(all } i, j \text{ in the group)}$$

that is, if the cost of obtaining a unit of the universal characteristic from a group good is the same for all group goods. Obviously the condition can be satisfied strictly only at one vector of relative prices for group goods. However, it will be approximately satisfied for all small price variations around this vector. This would seem an important property for operational application, since the conditions to be satisfied appear to be realistic enough. What they amount to is that if, for example, all automobiles possess a universal characteristic in addition to characteristics specific to automobiles, the amount of this character-istic, per dollar of automobile, is approximately the same from one automobile model to another.

It seems reasonable to assume that unless specific data are available, the content of universal characteristics among goods in a group is, per dollar spent, approximately the same for all goods in the group. If this and earlier conditions about the group being a minor contributor to the total amount of universal characteristic are satisfied, the feasible set in C'-space (group characteristics space) is closely approximated in shape by simply ignoring the effect of the universal characteristic and treating the group in isolation.

We have carried out the analysis for the case in which there is a single good outside the group, possessing only the universal characteristic. Without actually performing the more general analysis, it seems obvious that the generalization to many goods possessing the universal characteristic (along with other characteristics), and to more than one universal characteristic, will show the following points to be valid:

(1) The feasible set in C'-space is a contour of the overall feasible set in which all exogenous characteristics (that is, all characteristics other than those specific to the group in question) are constant.

(2) The exogenous characteristics are to be obtained efficiently so that the cost of obtaining the universal characteristic outside the group means the least cost of doing so, subject to obtaining the requisite quantities of other exogenous characteristics.

(3) With multiple universal characteristics the condition for uniform price distortion within a group will require the costs of obtaining each of the universal characteristics to be the same for all goods in the group. If the uniformity exists for one universal characteristic, it is guaranteed for the others if the technical coefficients are such that every good in the group possesses the various universal characteristics in the same proportions.

(4) With multiple universal characteristics and several groups, the uniform distortion requirement will require that the goods in each group possess the various universal characteristics in the same proportions, but the proportions may vary from group to group.

Concerning the preference functions, it is obvious that those of the Cobb-Douglas type, which are multiplicatively separable in all possible ways, will satisfy requirements.

8.5   A Small Group in a Large Universe

In the preceding section we examined the effect of a universal characteristic and showed that we could ignore it if we could assume approximately equal distortion to prices over a group. An alternative is to consider the conditions under which we can ignore the distortions altogether.

In the simple model with two group characteristics, one universal characteristic and one good outside the group which possessed only the universal characteristic, we showed that the feasible set in C'-space is obtained by using adjusted prices which requires that the market price of the ith group good be reduced by a percentage

$$\frac{p_4}{p_i} \cdot \frac{b_{3i}}{b_{34}}$$

When top and bottom are multiplied by k (the unadjusted budget) and rearranged, the percentage distortion becomes

$$\frac{kb_{3i}/p_i}{kb_{34}/p_4}$$

Now kb_{3i}/p_i is the quantity of universal characteristic obtained by spending the whole budget on the ith good. The denominator of the fraction is the quantity of universal characteristic obtained by spending the whole budget on G_4 (the good outside the group). If this ratio is very small, the percentage distortion is close to zero and market prices can be used as a close approximation to adjusted prices. At the same time the ratio as formulated above provides a "natural" description for the condition that it be very small.

A group of goods is defined as small in relation to the universe of goods if the maximum quantity of a universal characteristic that can be obtained by spending the whole budget on the group is small in relation to the maximum quantity of the universal characteristic that can be obtained by spending the whole budget outside the group. If a group is sufficiently small in the above sense, the price distortions due to the universal good can be neglected and the group can be analyzed in terms of the group characteristics as though the group were the whole universe. As in the previous analysis there is a subsidiary condition that is assumed to be satisfied, namely, that all the characteristics collections in which the consumer is interested include a quantity of the universal characteristic greater than can be obtained from the group goods alone, but less than could be obtained outside the group.

It is obvious from the analysis of the small group that the "universal characteristic" does not have to be possessed by all goods. It does not even need to be possessed by all goods in the group since the analysis does not depend on uniform distortion of price over the group, but on negligible distortion. We can consider a characteristic as "universal" for small group analysis if the maximum contribution of the group to the consumer's desired quantity of this characteristic is very small.

CHAPTER 9

RELEVANT CHARACTERISTICS:
A PRIORI CRITERIA

9.1 The Notion of a Relevant Characteristic

It is clear that if we count as a characteristic every property of a good that is objectively observable, the number of such "characteristics" approaches the infinite. On the other hand, our basic model and its analysis depend on the relationship between the number of goods and the number of characteristics, and its operational use depends on being able to confine our attention to a relatively small number of characteristics. Indeed, one of the most obvious uses of the model is in the analysis of product differentiates provided this can be done in terms of a smaller number of characteristics than of goods. Once the number of characteristics is as great as the number of goods, the model presented here has no great superiority over the traditional model (into which it then easily transforms), except in the discussion of new differentiates.

All the previous discussion of our theory has implicitly assumed that we can concern ourselves only with relevant characteristics. The time has arrived to consider the difficult problem of defining relevance and determining criteria for relevance. A characteristic is "relevant" to a situation (by which we mean the relationship of a consumer or consumers to a set of goods) if ignoring its existence would lead to different predictions about the choice or ordering of the goods by the consumers. In Chapter 10 we shall take up the question of how market data might be used to determine whether a given characteristic is proved relevant or not in a real situation. Even then, we need some a priori methods for eliminating characteristics from the set of those considered likely to be relevant. Common sense, for example, suggests that the serial number of an automobile will be an irrelevant characteristic although it is an objectively observable property, but we need a more formal set of criteria for most cases.

Characteristics bear a double relation to any situation. On the one hand, characteristics are technically related to goods through the characteristics–goods relationship or consumption technology. On the other hand, they have a human relationship to the consumers involved in the situation through the characteristics–people relationship, embodied in preferences. Although the two relationships cannot be entirely separated, we shall find it extremely useful to divide the criteria for irrelevance into those which are concerned mainly with the structure of technology and those which are concerned mainly with the structure of preferences. A characteristic may be ruled out as irrelevant for primarily technical reasons or for primarily human reasons.

We shall confine our attention to the analysis of a group since that is the context in which operational application will certainly take place. Thus we shall mean, by irrelevant, *irrelevant to the analysis of the group*.

9.2   Technical Irrelevance

From the analysis of the previous chapter we can immediately state one important criterion:

Universal characteristics are irrelevant to the small group.

This criterion holds for the modified definition of a universal characteristic, namely, that the group's total contribution of this characteristic be small compared to the contribution from goods outside the group, over the range of characteristics collections with which the analysis is concerned. If the group cannot be considered sufficiently small, in terms of its share in the total contribution of a universal characteristic, we can draw on the stronger condition, also developed in Chapter 8:

A universal characteristic is irrelevant to the group if the content of this characteristic, per dollar spent, is approximately uniform over goods in the group.

Both these criteria for irrelevance require the satisfaction of certain subsidiary conditions and also conditions on preferences. The second criterion obviously holds only if relative prices of group goods remain within a certain range. In spite of these conditions, the criteria are potentially of great use for practical application.

We shall assume, for practical uses, that our analysis is confined to groups which satisfy one or the other of these conditions and that, as a consequence, all universal characteristics (which we shall take to mean all characteristics not confined to group goods) can be regarded as irrelevant. Thus we shall turn our attention to criteria for irrelevance among group characteristics alone.

First we can introduce a simple criterion which, although not consistent with a strictly linear technology, is undoubtedly very useful in practice:

A characteristic which is invariant over the group is irrelevant.

By "invariant" here we mean either a characteristic of the (0, 1) kind which is simply present or absent or a quantitative characteristic which, owing to some kind of technical saturation, can be possessed only up to some maximum amount. In the earlier days of automobiles ease of starting was a variable characteristic and therefore possibly relevant. Contemporary model cars are all started easily, and the characteristic is invariant by saturation. Invariance and linearity are obviously inconsistent, but the technology may well be linear in all but the invariant characteristics, and therefore in the relevant characteristics.

Assuming that the technology, after ignoring invariant characteristics, is linear, we have another criterion, that of linear dependence in the technology. If the technology consists of r presumed relevant characteristics and n ($\geq r$) goods, the technology matrix may be of some rank less than r, say rank s. This implies that all the independent information in the technology is contained in any s rows, that is, that the amounts of $r - s$ of the characteristics can be predicted from knowledge of the amounts of the remaining s. In a sense $r - s$ of the characteristics are redundant.

In the simplest case of linear dependence one row of the technology matrix is the same as, or a scalar multiple of, some other row. Consider a three-good, three-characteristic model with technology matrix:

$$\begin{bmatrix} b_{11} & b_{12} & b_{13} \\ b_{21} & b_{22} & b_{23} \\ \mu b_{21} & \mu b_{22} & \mu b_{23} \end{bmatrix}$$

Since the coefficients for characteristic 3 (the bottom row) are equal to μ times the coefficients for characteristic 2, the amount of z_1 provided by any collection of the goods will be exactly μ times the amount of z_2. Alternatively, since there is no implied cause-effect priority, the amount of z_2 will be exactly $1/\mu$ times the amount of z_3.

Since the technology matrix has rank 2 only, the feasible set in C-space will be in a subspace of dimension 2—a plane in this case. A

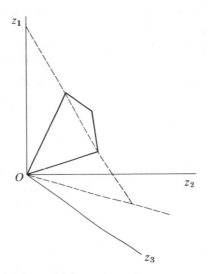

Figure 9.1. Technology with linear dependence

typical feasible set for this technology is shown in Figure 9.1. It will lie in a vertical plane (as drawn, with z_1, vertical) containing the z_1, axis and intersecting the z_2z_3 plane between the z_2 and z_3 axes along a line which divides the angle z_2Oz_3 in a ratio which depends on the value of μ. Obviously if $\mu = 1$, the plane will be at 45° to both Oz_2 and Oz_3. We can always choose the units of characteristic z_3 so that $\mu = 1$, and we shall suppose this to have been done henceforth, so that $z_3 = z_2$.

Although the feasible set is in two dimensions, it is not in either the z_1z_2 or z_2z_3 plane. The two-dimension property of the feasible set is not equivalent merely to ignoring z_2 or z_3. Strictly speaking, we can reduce the feasible set to one in two dimensions by introducing a new characteristic $\zeta = z_2 = z_3$, then analyzing the model in ζ-space. However, the feasible set in ζ-space will look exactly as it would if we were to draw it in $z_1 z_2$ space, ignoring the existence of z_3 altogether.

It will not, however, be the same thing from the consumer's point of view. Suppose the consumer has utility function $u(z_1, z_2, z_3)$, and we consider the point $[\bar{z}_1, \bar{\zeta}]$. To ignore z_3 altogether is associating with this point the preference level $u(\bar{z}_1, \bar{\zeta}, ?)$, while the correct preference level is given by $u(\bar{z}_1, \bar{\zeta}, \bar{\zeta})$. For the Cobb-Douglas function $u = z_1{}^\alpha z_2{}^\beta z_3{}^\gamma$, ignoring z_3 is equivalent to taking the function to be $u = z_1{}^\alpha \zeta^b$ instead of $u = z^\alpha \zeta^\beta \zeta^\beta = z_1{}^\alpha \zeta^{\beta+\gamma}$. Since the marginal rate of substitution between z_1 and z_2 will appear to be proportional to α/β when z_3 is ignored, instead of $\alpha/\beta + \gamma$, the predicted behavior will be incorrect.

In general, we do not have prior information concerning complete preferences, and any derivation of revealed preference from market behavior based on ignoring z_3 will automatically give z_2 the "weight" appropriate to both itself and z_3, so the problem of the preference function is of little practical importance. In many cases, of course, it will be appropriate to assume that characteristics technically related in this way are also related in the view of the consumer so that he reacts to any one of the related characteristics, not to each of them separately. This assumption is clearly appropriate if all the related "characteristics" are, in a sense, different indicators of the same fundamental property from the consumer's point of view—different indexes of "comfort" or "convenience" or "size."

If two or more characteristics are possessed by all goods in fixed ratio to each other, we can treat all but one of them as irrelevant. However, if prior information concerning complete preferences is available, the preference function must be suitably transformed in some cases.

It seems appropriate to refer to characteristics rejected on this criterion as *technically redundant*. We can extend the analysis to any number of dimensions, of course. We can also extend it to cover cases in which a particular characteristic is not possessed by all goods in a fixed ratio to some other characteristic, but its content can be expressed as a linear combination of other characteristics, with the same weights for all goods.

Consider, for example, the three-good, three-characteristic technology

$$\begin{bmatrix} 3 & 1 & 2 \\ 1 & 3 & 2 \\ 1\frac{2}{3} & 2\frac{1}{3} & 2 \end{bmatrix}$$

The coefficient for the third characteristic is the weighted average of the coefficient for the other two (with weights 1/3, 2/3) in each case. Thus, for any goods collection giving amounts z_1, z_2 of the first two characteristics, the amount of the third characteristic will ge given by

$$z_3 = \tfrac{1}{3}z_1 + \tfrac{2}{3}z_2$$

The rank of this matrix is 2, and the feasible set is planar. In principle we could ignore z_3 after transforming the utility function

$$u(z_1, z_2, z_3) = u(z_1, z_2, \tfrac{1}{3}z_1 + \tfrac{2}{3}z_2) = v(z_1, z_2)$$

Complex linear dependence in the consumption technology is not likely to be discovered by simple a priori investigation. Since it has no intuitive appeal as to interpretation, and leads to complex transformations of simple preference functions, we shall generally ignore it.

For non-linear technologies it is not difficult to derive conditions for technical redundance analogous to the simple case in the linear technology. In general, a characteristic is technically redundant if it is in constant ratio to another characteristic for all quantities of all goods. In practical application it is reasonable to require only approximation to a fixed technical relationship in order to use the redundance criterion. Thus, with minimal constraint on individual preferences (which are unknown in practical situations), we have shown that characteristics can usually be ruled out as irrelevant for group analysis if they are: (i) universal characteristics; (ii) invariant over the group; (iii) technically redundant over the group.

The first criterion rules out characteristics not confined to the group, the second rules out characteristics which do not vary over the group, the third rules out characteristics which are in technically fixed proportions to other characteristics, including alternative indicators of the same basic property. Most of these criteria can be used, in the initial stages of a problem at least, to quickly eliminate characteristics by drawing on relatively casual observation of the group and its relationship to the goods universe.

9.3 Human Irrelevance

As pointed out above, characteristics may be relevant or irrelevant because of their relationships to goods or their relationships to people. It is the latter set of relationships which now concern us.

In the earlier marginalists goods were considered to be related to people because they satisfied "wants." This is no place for a discussion of what these writers really meant by "wants." It is sufficient that they were considered entirely human properties that were, in some way, matched with or "satisfied" by certain goods and that preferences depended on the relationship between wants and the properties of goods. It was not supposed by these writers that there was a one-to-one correspondence between wants and goods. On the contrary, it was generally assumed that a particular good could satisfy a large number of wants, which were arranged in a hierarchy so that the first quantity of the goods satisfied the most urgent want, the next quantity the next more urgent, and so on. Thus Menger[1] describes the isolated farmer allocating corn first for his own, then his family's basic survival, then for above survival food, then for seed, then for beer, then for fattening livestock, and so on.

Characteristics, in our model, are observable properties of goods, but their relevance to people lies in their ability to generate some response (perhaps negative) in consumers. In this sense we could refer to a characteristic as "satisfying wants," in some fashion. Because of its conceptual redundance we shall generally avoid this way of stating the relationship, but there is an undoubted similarity to what the earlier writers had in mind. Since a characteristic is only a single property of a good, which may possess many, there is a closer matching of single characteristics with single psychological aims than there is of single goods.

In terms of people-characteristics relationships we can state the simplest and most obvious criterion for irrelevance:

A characteristic is totally irrelevant if it does not appear in consumers' preference functions ("satisfies no wants"), either positively or negatively.

Since we are concerned with aggregate market behavior in typical applications of the model it is sufficient for total irrelevance that a characteristic does not appear in the preferences of a large proportion of the consumer population. We can often also rule out a characteristic that has a very low weight in preferences (a very low exponent, in the Cobb-Douglas form) relative to the weights of other characteristics. Note that, for a group, a characteristic whose content in the group goods might be described as not going far towards "satisfying a want," in relation to other goods, conforms to the earlier idea of a universal

[1] Karl Menger, *Principles of Economics*, 1871. English translation, 1950.

characteristic and is so ruled out. Assuming totally irrelevant characteristics to have been eliminated, we turn to seek guidance as to the possibility of some characteristics being irrelevant to consumers under some
identifiable circumstances. This leads to ideas of hierarchy, satiation,
and dominance.

A prominent feature of the "wants" approach, which we wish to
take up, is *hierarchy*. One of Menger's examples has already been given,
and there are many others. Georgescu-Roegen[2] points to examples in
the writings of Plato, Jevons, Wieser, Walras, Marshall, Pareto, and
Knight. At the behavioral level there are hierarchical implications in
Engel's law and other well-established relationships between income
and the expenditure on a particular class of goods. Recently Paroush
has found consistency in the order in which consumers acquire durables,
again with hierarchical implications.

Hierarchy in goods does not necessarily represent an underlying
hierarchy of wants, since technical relationships may also be involved,
especially in the case of durable goods.[3] A person may prefer sailing
to driving, yet may buy a car before a boat because, without a car, he
cannot transport the boat to water but, without a boat, he can still use
his car. Characteristics, like goods, may be subject to technical com-
plementarities that give hierarchical properties without any psychological implications. We can also have a hierarchy of characteristics (for
psychological reasons) without any goods hierarchy being manifest,
because the characteristics in question are not confined to an easily
identifiable group of goods.

9.4 Satiation Effects

Closely associated with the idea of a hierarchy of wants in some kind of
satiation effect. In the original arguments of Menger and other writers
in the same vein the hierarchy was relevant because the consumer
satisfied his wants in order of importance. Obviously, unless the most
important want was satiable, the next most important would be
irrelevant. Jevons, for example, wrote:[4] "The satisfaction of a lower
want . . . merely permits the higher want to manifest itself." In the

[2] N. Georgescu-Roegen, *Analytical Economics, Issues and Problems*, Harvard, 1966.
[3] J. Paroush, "The order of acquisition of consumer durables," *Econometrica*, Vol.
33, pp. 225–35, 1965.
[4] W. Stanley Jevons, *The Theory of Political Economy* (4th Ed.), London, 1924, p. 54.

traditional analysis of consumer behavior (meaning the now traditional analysis, developed well after Jevons and Menger), satiation appears only negatively as the non-satiation postulate built into formal versions of the theory. Non-satiation in the normal form is convenient rather than necessary, although non-satiation over the feasible region is necessary to ensure the existence of a competitive equilibrium.

Strong non-satiation (no satiation of any good) is easy enough to live with in the coarse-structure context of traditional theory, where the "goods" are really conceived of as aggregates. In the characteristics model, with its special adaptability to fine-structure situations like the markets for differentiated products, we can depend much less on broad ideas of smoothness and continuity. We need, in particular, to examine closely such phenomena as satiation.

A satiation relationship between a consumer and a characteristic implies that the consumer has no positive interest in further quantities of the characteristic. This may mean either of two things, leading to a classification of satiation into two types. The consumer may have (i) zero interest in further quantities of the characteristic or (ii) a negative interest in further quantities. We can illustrate the two types from a diet example. Consider a sophisticated consumer whose choice is restricted to choice of food only, who considers (among other things) the nutritive content of his food, and who needs (and knows he needs) a daily intake of 2500 calories and 5000 units of vitamin A. Thus, among the various characteristics of his food, he seeks to attain these particular levels of the nutrients.

Once he has obtained 5000 units of vitamin A, he has no further interest in this characteristic. Assuming that amounts of vitamin A above 5000 units have no effects, good or bad, we can assume the consumer has zero interest in further quantities. We shall refer to this type of satiation, where the consumer simply ceases to note the characteristic once the minimum level has been attained, as *open satiation*.

But once the consumer has attained 2500 calories he may well be anxious to avoid gaining weight and so may have a negative interest in further calories. This does not imply that he will not, under any circumstances, consume further calories, merely that he will do so only if the excess food contains other characteristics (flavor, for example) in which he retains a positive interest. We shall refer to this type of satiation, in which a characteristic changes from being desirable to being undesirable, as *closed satiation*.

More formally, for a consumer's world of two characteristics z_1 and z_2, the consumer reaches:

(1) *Open satiation* at level $\bar{z}_2$ for characteristic z_2 if, for any characteristics collections Z, Z' such that

$$z_1 = z_1'$$
$$z_2, z_2' \geqq \bar{z}_2$$

we have ZIZ', whatever the relationship of z_2, z_2'.

(2) *Closed satiation* at level $\bar{z}_2$ for characteristic z_2 if, (a) for any collections Z, Z' such that

$$z_1 = z_1'$$
$$z_2 > z_2' \geqq \bar{z}_2$$

we have $Z'PZ$, and (b) for any collections Z, Z' such that

$$z_1 = z_1'$$
$$z_2 < z_2' \leqq \bar{z}_2$$

we have $Z'\bar{P}Z$ (that is, Z preferred or indifferent to Z').

Representative indifference maps illustrating the two types of satiation for the two-characteristic model are shown in Figure 9.2. In the open satiation case [Figure 9.2(a)] the indifference curves are vertical above the line $z_2 = \bar{z}_2$, while in the closed satiation case [Figure 9.2(b)] they have a positive slope in this region. In some instances (including the calorie example already given) it may be more realistic to assume that open satiation is reached at one level, and closed satiation at a higher level. The consumer may, for example, decide he has approximately enough calories at 2000 and lose interest in them so long as he does not exceed 3000, at which level his negative reaction starts. This gives a region of open satiation or *neutral zone* with respect to the characteristics, as illustrated in Figure 9.3.

Satiation is generally assumed to be open satiation in the economics literature. Stigler's diet problem (a precursor of the characteristics approach as well as of linear programming) assumed open satiation, permitting a linear programming solution for minimum cost subject to minimum nutrient content, without worrying about excess nutrients. The "want satiation" of the early marginalists was, of course, open satiation. Any characteristic of a good concerned only with supplying a more urgent want was assumed to have zero effect on the satisfaction of less urgent wants.

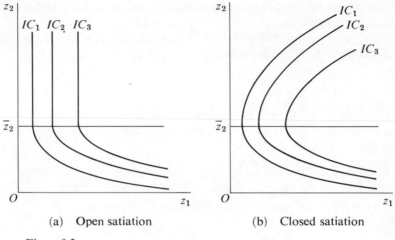

(a)   Open satiation   (b)   Closed satiation

Figure 9.2

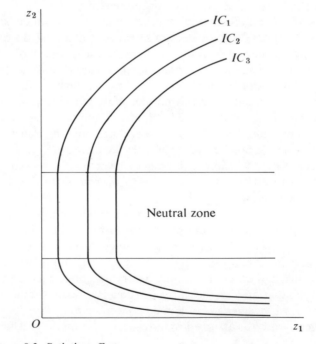

Figure 9.3. Satiation effects

Satiation with respect to a characteristic may or may not appear as a satiation effect with respect to a good. To investigate the relationship, consider the simple case of a two-characteristic model, in which one characteristic is subject to either open or closed satiation with respect to the consumer(s) in question. The other characteristic is assumed to be

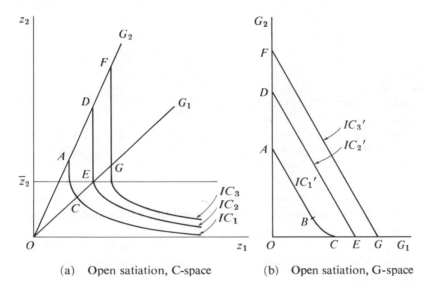

(a)   Open satiation, C-space   (b)   Open satiation, G-space

Figure 9.4

non-satiable. We shall consider a world of two goods, both of which possess both characteristics.

Figure 9.4 shows an illustration of the open satiation case. Figure 9.4(a) is drawn in C-space, with characteristics z_1 and z_2 measured along the axes. Characteristic z_2 is subject to open satiation at level $\bar{z}_2$. Rays OG_1, OG_2 represent the proportions in which the two characteristics are contained in goods G_1, G_2.

If we transform the diagram into G-space (hinging OG_1 and OG_2 about 0 until they are perpendicular), we obtain Figure 9.4(b). The sections of indifference curves (like FG) which are vertical in C-space have a negative slope in G-space, so that there is no satiation with respect to either of the goods. However, since the indifference curves for collections of goods which give amounts of z_2 above the satiation level are straight lines, choice subject to the typical budget constraint will give a corner solution in this region, either G_1 alone or G_2 alone, unless the budget line has exactly the same slope as FG.

In the satiation region we could predict which of the goods G_1 or G_2 would be chosen *without reference to* z_2. In the G-space diagram, point F (G_2 only) would be chosen if the budget line passed through F and some point on the G_1 axis to the left of G, such as E. Reference to Figure 9.4(a) shows that F has more z_1 than E. Similarly, if the budget line sloped from D to G in Figure 9.4(b), the consumer would choose point G, containing more z_1 than point D. Thus a characteristic becomes irrelevant in the region of open satiation with respect to it. In the example all consumer behavior in the region beyond DE in Figure 9.4(b) could be predicted from a knowledge of the content of z_1 in each of the goods and the relative prices.

Open satiation, therefore, does not necessarily lead to any satiation effects (even open satiation) on goods, but it does make a characteristic operationally irrelevant in the region of satiation. The characteristic will not, of course, be irrelevant below the satiation level. Thus, if all consumers are assumed to have approximately the same satiation relation to the characteristic, it may be relevant in a poor society below satiation but irrelevant in a rich society.

At high income levels, some characteristics may become irrelevant because of open satiation effects, At lower income levels, these characteristics may be relevant.

If there is closed satiation with respect to z_2, the situation with respect to goods is quite complex. Representative indifference curves showing three cases are given in Figure 9.5. In Figure 9.5(a) the indifference curve slopes positively above satiation, but with a slope steeper than that of OG_2 inside the attainable cone (defined by OG_2 and OG_1). Transformed into G-space, the portion AB of the indifference curve will have a negative slope, even though the slope is positive in C-space. There will be no satiation effect with respect to goods.

In Figure 9.5(b) the indifference curve is shown straight and parallel to OG_2 from the point A. Transformed into G-space, this portion of the indifference curve will be vertical, giving open satiation on G_2 but no satiation effects on G_1.

In Figure 9.5(c) the indifference curves slope over enough to cut OG_1. If both goods are assumed to have positive prices, any point to the northeast of C along IC_1 would be an inefficient choice, since a preferred position (on IC_2) could be obtained with less of both goods. C is

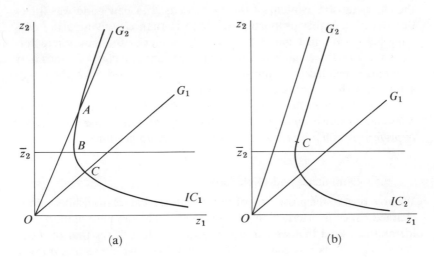

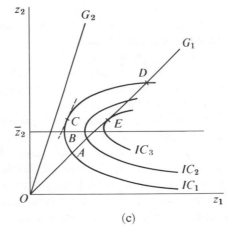

(c)

Figure 9.5. Closed satiation effects

the point on IC_1 at which the slope is the same as that of OG_2. In this case there is a most preferred goods collection (corresponding to the point E) giving satiation of *both* goods in the sense that with no budget constraint of any kind the consumer would choose only G_1 and that only up to the amount corresponding to the point E. With no budget constraint the consumer is subject to the technical constraint defined by the characteristics content of the two goods. If a new good was introduced with a higher proportion of z_1 to z_2 than G_1 (giving a ray OG_3 lying below OG_1 in Figure 9.5(c), the consumer's attainable characteristics set would be expanded. Thus a new variant of a class of goods may result in expanded consumption of those goods, although there was satiation with respect to existing goods of that class.

Closed satiation does not necessarily provide any criterion for irrelevance. It may complicate the analysis a great deal by causing switches in preferences on a characteristic from positive to negative.

9.5   Dominance and Hierarchy

We now turn to the possibility of using hierarchical relationships among characteristics as a criterion for relevance. The simplest notion of a hierarchical kind that we can apply to characteristics is that of *dominance* in preference. A characteristic is dominant within some group of characteristics, in some set of situations, if the consumer always prefers a collection with more of the dominant characteristic, whatever the amounts of the other characteristics.

Let us return to our diet example. For a starving man all other characteristics of food may be dominated by calorie content, interest in other nutrients being subordinated to the need to obtain sufficient calories for survival in the short run. An alcoholic may rank wines by their alcohol content alone, irrespective of any other characteristics. The alcoholic example is often used to illustrate lexicographical ordering. Dominance is a weaker assumption that lexicographical ordering, requiring, in effect, only that all words beginning with A come before all words beginning with B and not considering the ordering of words within the A-group. Operationally, dominance is observable, lexicographic ordering only so in rare instances.

Dominance, as in the diet example, may occur only over some region of choice. Consider the nutrition model, for we can illustrate many effects in it. Suppose that food has only two characteristics, calories and "flavor." A consumer is assumed to be given all non-food items in fixed quantities so that his choice context is confined to food.

We shall assume the following to be true of the characteristics-consumer relationship in this case:

(1) At very low calorie levels, calories are dominant.

(2) At medium calorie levels, flavor is relevant.

(3) There is a neutral zone with respect to calories—open satiation at one level, followed by closed satiation at a higher level.

(4) Flavor is non-satiable.

An indifferent map expressing the above properties would look like Figure 9.6. The lowest indifference curves would be horizontal (calories dominant), while higher ones would have a vertical segment (open

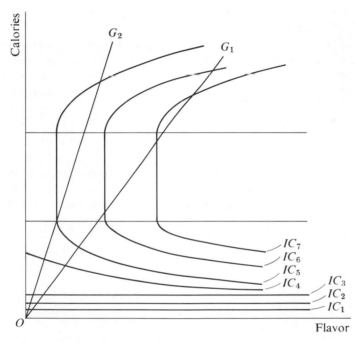

Figure 9.6. Dominance and satiation

satiation in the neutral zone) turning into a positive sloped segment (closed satiation).

If there were only two goods, G_2 having the higher ratio of calories to flavor, and the consumer faced a regular linear budget constraint, his choise would be determined in the following ways:

(1) At very low income levels he would be interested only in obtaining the most calories for his money. This would be determined from the calorie content of the two goods and their relative prices. Note that

he would not necessarily consume G_2, with the highest calorie/flavor ratio, He would consume the more flavorsome G_1 if that happened to have the highest calorie/outlay ratio at the market prices.

(2) In the next income bracket both calories and flavor count, and the content of both characteristics in both goods needs to be known.

(3) The next income bracket covers the neutral zone, with calories subject to open satiation. In effect, flavor is a dominant characteristic here, and choice will be decided by the flavor/outlay ratio.

(4) Finally, both characteristics count once more at high income levels, with calories regarded negatively.

Thus, in a single simple example, we see how the set of operationally relevant characteristics is reduced from two to one (a different one each time) at different income levels, while both characteristics are relevant (although one is first desirable then undesirable) at other income levels.

The conclusions to be drawn from our brief examination of an almost completely unexplored area are that hierarchial and dominance effects provide potential criteria for relevance and irrelevance. If nothing else they point to the important possibility that the set of operationally relevant characteristics may well depend on levels of real income due to satiation and hierarchy effects. Thus caution must be observed in transferring a successful analysis based on one particular set of relevant characteristics to a different socio-economic context.

CHAPTER 10

REVEALED RELEVANCE, WITH AN APPLICATION TO THE UNITED STATES AUTOMOBILE MARKET

10.1 The Problem

In Chapter 9 we discussed criteria for eliminating characteristics as irrelevant on various ex ante grounds, some based on the consumption technology and some on the structure of preferences. Generally speaking, we can usually presume to possess information sufficient to apply those criteria which depend on the technology and some of the broader criteria which depend on preferences. We do not, however, possess detailed information on individual preferences.

The aim of revealed relevance techniques is to use observed market data to deduce something about whether certain characteristics are or are not relevant in the preference sense—that is, whether consumers appear to react to these characteristics or not. All the techniques are based on the simple principle of efficient choice, discussed at length in Chapters 2, 3, and 4. We can restate the principle in the form in which we shall use it here:

No consumer will choose an inefficient goods collection that is, one which possesses less of some characteristic and no more of others than some other available collection.

Thus a good which is actually sold cannot be part of an inefficient

collection in the above sense. If it appears to be so, it is because we are
not taking into account the proper set of relevant characteristics.

We shall use the shorthand of referring to a good as inefficient if it
does not appear in any efficient collection. The above statement assumes
all characteristics to be positively desired. It can be modified for negative characteristics. In practical applications we may wish to be a little
flexible with respect to the phrase "no consumer . . ." and consider that
when an apparently inefficient good is actually sold, but sold in small
quantities (especially if it is widely regarded as a market flop), it does
not provide a case for modifying our preliminary set of characteristics.

The ideal case, of course, would be one in which a model or price
change resulted in a good becoming inefficient while the market data
showed the sales declining sharply (even if not to zero). This would both
confirm the usefulness of the general model and suggest that we had
picked the appropriate set of relevant characteristics.

To develop criteria for revealed relevance, we need to investigate the
following:

(1) What happens when we ignore a characteristic that is actually
relevant to choice.

(2) What happens if we include a characteristic which is technically
relevant but to which consumers have no reaction.

We shall now proceed to these investigations. The linear model is
assumed unless otherwise specified. The analysis applies equally to the
whole consumption universe or to the set of relevant characteristics for
a group.

10.2   Ignoring Relevant Characteristics

Consider a simple linear model of three goods and three characteristics
in which the technology and prices are such that all three goods are
efficient. There is no technical redundancy, so the feasible set in C-space
does not reduce to one of two dimensions. The technology matrix will
be 3×3.

$$\begin{bmatrix} b_{11} & b_{12} & b_{13} \\ b_{21} & b_{22} & b_{23} \\ b_{31} & b_{32} & b_{33} \end{bmatrix}$$

Under these conditions the feasible set in C-space must be a triangular facet with a positive normal, and one such possibility is shown in Figure 10.1.

Now suppose we simply ignore characteristic z_3. In algebraic terms this is equivalent to incorrectly supposing all the entries in the third row of the technology matrix to be zero, giving the false matrix:

$$\begin{bmatrix} b_{11} & b_{12} & b_{13} \\ b_{21} & b_{22} & b_{23} \\ 0 & 0 & 0 \end{bmatrix}$$

Geometrically, it is equivalent to simply projecting the feasible set of Figure 10.1 vertically on to the $z_1 z_2$ plane. This will give the false

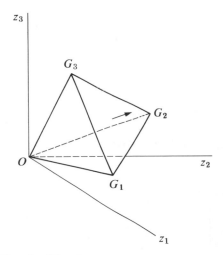

Figure 10.1. True feasible set

feasible set in $z_1 z_2$ space of Figure 10.2. If the false feasible set of Figure 10.2 was taken for the true feasible set, we would conclude that G_3 was inefficient and thus predict that G_3 would not be sold.

On the other hand, the true feasible set might be like that of Figure 10.3. Ignoring characteristic z_3 in this case would give the false feasible set of Figure 10.4. G_3 would no longer be inefficient, and there would be no prediction that G_3 would not be sold.

We could distinguish between predictions of the true feasible set

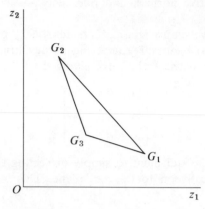

Figure 10.2. False feasible set

and the false feasible set even in this case, however. From the false feasible set we would predict:

(1) No individual consumer would consume *both* G_1 and G_3, only combinations G_1–G_2 or G_2–G_3.

(2) No individual consumer would consume all three goods simultaneously.

Neither of these predictions would be made from the true feasible

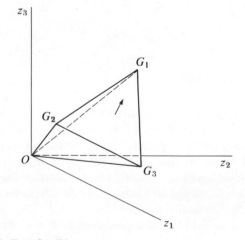

Figure 10.3. True feasible set

set. Since the true feasible set is a facet we would expect a considerable proportion of the consumers to purchase all three goods, given a more or less uniform preference distribution.

There is an important difference between these two cases. In the first case (Figures 10.1 and 10.2) the prediction of the false feasible set (G_3 will not be sold) is a prediction concerning aggregate market behavior and can be falsified by aggregate market data. In the second

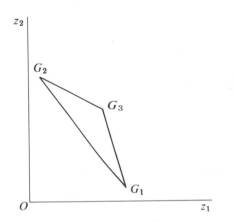

Figure 10.4. False feasible set

case (Figures 10.3 and 10.4) the prediction concerns individual behavior and cannot be falsified by aggregate market data. Evidence that all three goods are sold in no way contradicts a prediction that no individual consumer will buy all three.

Aggregate market data can, however, be used in an extreme version of the second case. Suppose that in Figure 10.3 the price of G_3 falls sufficiently for G_3 to dominate G_1 and G_2 in true C-space, as shown in Figure 10.5(a). That is, by spending the whole budget on G_3, more of z_3 as well as z_1 and z_2 can be obtained than from some combinations of G_1 and G_2, but not more of z_1 and z_2 than from G_1 and G_2 individually. Then the false feasible set will be of the same kind as that in Figure 10.4, and is shown in Figure 10.5(b). The false feasible set will predict that G_1 and G_2 will actually be sold (assuming well-distributed preferences), but the true feasible set will predict sale of G_3 only. This case is of somewhat doubtful utility, partly because it depends on an extreme market situation (dominance of general goods by one other good) and partly because it depends on negative evidence (goods which are predicted as being sold and are not).

Equivalent negative evidence would appear in the extreme case if the range of preferences was narrow, so that collections of characteristics corresponding to G_1 and G_2 were not of interest to consumers, even if the false feasible set correctly described the situation. We could eliminate a

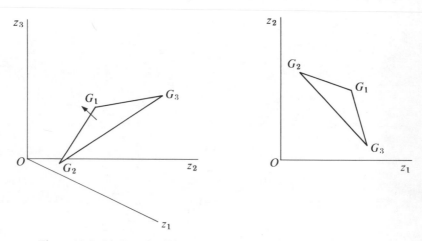

Figure 10.5. (a) True feasible set, (b) False feasible set

false reading on this count if there were other goods more extreme than G_1 and G_2—another good to the northwest of G_2 in Figure 10.4 and another to the southeast of G_1—which were actually sold.

The three-good three-characteristic analysis can, of course, be generalized. With more characteristics the efficiency-inefficiency relationship beomes more complex, and, in a practical case, inefficient goods would need to be found by linear programming methods. We can, however, lay down the guiding principles for detecting whether effective characteristics have been ignored.

Assuming a linear model with adequate knowledge of the consumption technology, we compute the feasible set for a given market situation in terms of some set of s characteristics. The revealed relevance criteria then become:

(1) A sufficient condition for concluding that an effective characteristic is missing is that a good which is inefficient in terms of s characteristics is actually sold. This requires only aggregate market data.

However, even if an effective characteristic is missing, it is possible for all good to be efficient in terms of only s characteristics, so the criterion is sufficient only, and not necessary.

(2) A sufficient condition for concluding that an effective characteristic is missing is that *individuals* consume more than s different goods. This requires data on individual market behavior and cannot be used for aggregate data only. It may be applicable in cases in which (1) is useless (no goods inefficient in terms of s characteristics). In principle it is also necessary and sufficient if (a) preferences are widely distributed over the whole of C-space and (b) there is no dominance in the market. Under these conditions the number of effective characteristics is the maximum number of different goods consumed by any individual. In practice it would be dangerous to rely on the necessity property, even if data were available, because the preference distribution and dominance properties may not be satisfied.

(3) A further criterion for close scrutiny of the set of characteristics is present when a good actually dominates the market but is not shown to be dominant in terms of s characteristics. However, we shall see in the next section, the appropriate conclusion is not necessarily that a relevant characteristic is missing, even if widely distributed preferences can be assumed.

10.3   Inserting Irrelevant Characteristics

We now turn to the problem which is a kind of inverse to that discussed in the previous section, namely, what happens if we include a characteristic that is irrelevant to all consumers. It is assumed that the characteristic is not technically irrelevant or redundant, that it is a real independent characteristic that happens to be of no interest to consumers. For Cobb-Douglas preferences this implies that the associated exponent is zero for all consumers.

The analysis consists basically of inverting the analysis of the previous section. We now suppose that the true situation is represented by three goods and two characteristics, and that we falsely assume a third characteristic to be relevant. Although we shall use the term "false feasible set" for the three-characteristic feasible set, to remain uniform with the terminology of the previous section, the feasible set is not really false (since we assume all characteristics to be real) but irrelevant to actual choice. The "falsity" is in the deductions made by assuming that

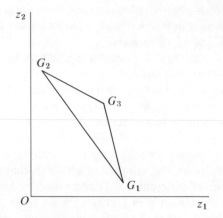

Figure 10.6. True feasible set

the situation is one in which the feasible set is in three characteristics, all of which count.

If the three goods are all efficient in the given market situation the true feasible set will be like that of Figure 10.6. Since the third character-istic is ineffective, the false feasible set will be related to the true feasible set in a manner inverse to that of the previous section. That is, the false feasible set will necessarily be one whose projection on the z_1z_2 plane

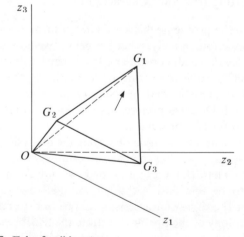

Figure 10.7. False feasible set

gives the pattern of Figure 10.6. Thus the false feasible set corresponding to Figure 10.6 will be that shown in Figure 10.7.

In this case, the false feasible set will predict that all three goods will be consumed by some individuals, and combinations of G_1-G_2 by others (assuming widely distributed preferences), whereas the true feasible set will predict no simultaneous consumption of all three goods and no G_1-G_2 combinations. The criterion for determining that z_3 is

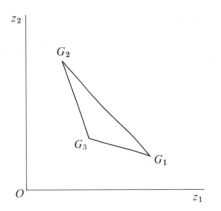

Figure 10.8. True feasible set

irrelevant thus depends on individual market behavior and widely distributed preferences.

When the true feasible set is like that of Figure 10.8, the false feasible set will be like that of Figure 10.9. The false feasible set will predict that G_3 will be sold, while the true feasible set predicts that it is inefficient and will not be sold. The criterion in this case depends on aggregate data alone, and there are no preference distribution problems of importance, but it still depends on negative evidence. To call the conditions we derive from the above criteria "sufficient" is going too far because of the rather negative nature of the evidence needed, so we shall refer to them simply as "presumptive."

Finally, let us look at the case of actual market dominance. If the true feasible set was as shown in Figure 10.10, G_3 would dominate G_1 and G_2 and only G_3 would actually be sold. This set would be consistent with the false feasible set of Figure 10.11, in which there is no

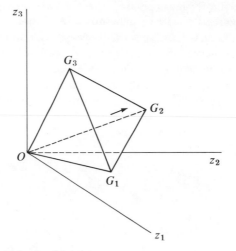

Figure 10.9. False feasible set

dominance. But we showed in the last section that a prediction of no
dominance that would be falsified by actual dominance could also
occur if there were too few characteristics in the set chosen as relevant,
as well as too many. All that we can conclude from the dominance case
is that the original set of relevant characteristics need to be looked at
again.

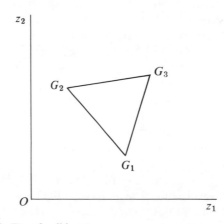

Figure 10.10. True feasible set

The criteria for irrelevance are inherently weaker than those for determining whether a relevant characteristic is missing:

(1) A presumptive condition for the existence of irrelevant characteristics in the chosen set of s characteristics is that no individual consumes as many as s different goods. This is a weak condition and depends on individual market data.

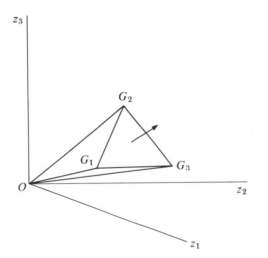

Figure 10.11. False feasible set

(2) A presumptive condition for the existence of irrelevant chatacteristics is that some good, predicted as efficient in terms of s characteristics, is not actually sold. Although this requires aggregate market data only, its negative form makes it weak.

(3) The existence of actual dominance, where no dominance is predicted from the chosen characteristics, suggests reassessment of the chosen set. This case is consistent with both too few and too many characteristics in the chosen set.

10.4   Revealed Relevance in the United States Automobile Market

To test the general feasibility of the revealed relevance approach and to test the general hypothesis, implicit throughout the book, that the

analysis of product differentiates can be carried out with fewer characteristics than goods, a simple analysis has been made of the automobile
market in the United States.

The automobile market seems an obvious one to study. The product
differentiates (models) are clearly defined and codified, and the wide
interest in the problem of choosing an automobile has led to the
publishing of automobile test reports by several organizations. We

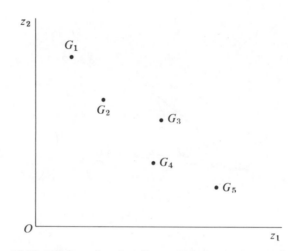

Figure 10.12. Efficiency frontier, discrete case

cannot, however, make the automobile market fit our standard model
because an automobile purchase is a "one-shot" decision. A consumer
sets out, except in very special cases, to buy a single automobile. Thus
he must find his optimal collection of characteristics in a single good,
not in a combination. The efficiency frontier becomes a set of discrete
points, as shown in Figure 10.12.

Each point represents the characteristics of one car of the particular
model. Since there are no combinations represented by lines joining the
points on the frontier, efficiency comparisons involve discrete points
only. Thus point G_2 in the diagram cannot be asserted to be inefficient,
as it could be if points on the line joining G_1 and G_3 were feasible. But
G_4 is inefficient because there is another discrete point (G_3) with more of
both characteristics.

In the discrete case efficiency comparisons involve checking whether there is any good having more of at least one, and no less of any other, characteristic than the good in question. If the answer is affirmative the good is inefficient. In the revealed relevance context, where we assume all goods efficient (if actually sold) and search for relevant characteristics, we know we are lacking a relevant characteristic if we can find any goods so related that one appears inefficient in terms of our original choice of characteristics.

Inefficiency comparisons in the discrete case do not involve linear programming solutions, as when combinations are possible, but involve making all possible pairwise comparisons between discrete points.

Although we have a much weaker test for efficiency, real or apparent, in the discrete case, we pick up a very useful incidental effect. Without combinations, we do not need to measure characteristics, merely to rank them. In the discrete case efficiency comparisons depend only on whether one good has more or less of a characteristic than another, not on the amount of the difference. Thus it is sufficient that we can rank the goods in terms of each of the characteristics. We cannot use measure information in this case, even if we have it.

Since discrete case comparisons are based on rankings and pairwise comparisons, we can note the general dimensions of our potential set of relevant characteristics. With n goods, there are $n!$ possible rank orderings. In other words, it would be possible to have $n!$ different characteristics, with the ranking of the goods different for each characteristic. For any pair of goods, the first would be ranked above the second in exactly half the rankings, below in the other half. Thus it is possible that we could have $\frac{1}{2}n!$ different characteristics for a group of n goods and still have no good having less of all characteristics than some other good. The maximum number of relevant characteristics that we could appear to have is thus $\frac{1}{2}n!$, or 360 for a group of only 6 goods. If combinations are possible, a maximum of n relevant characteristics— 6 for 6 goods—is all that is required.

The minimum number of relevant characteristics is just 2, for groups of any size. This is because if goods are ranked in some order with respect to characteristic 1 and in the exact reverse order for characteristic 2, all pairwise comparisons will show one good ranked higher with respect to characteristic 1, the other with respect to characteristic 2. Because rank information is all that can be used, there is no problem in obtaining information for the automobile market. There are many test reports which rank various car models with respect to potentially relevant characteristics. Problems of a priori choice are largely eliminated because the testing organizations have already selected those things about automobiles that are likely to be of interest to consumers.

What about price and the budget constraint? This is also simplified by the one-shot nature of the decision, and the discrete quantity decision. We are interested in relationships among models and can therefore assume the consumer has set out to buy just one car. Price is clearly relevant, but we can treat it as though it were a characteristic on the presumption that, if two models ranked equally in all characteristics, the cheaper would be purchased, at least within the group. Thus being cheaper is a rankable characteristic that we can treat as any other.

The actual analysis is based on the test reports in *Consumer Reports* (Consumers Union) for 1969 model cars. These reports rate the car models with respect to various properties[1] which we take as our presumptive set of characteristics. The characteristics are:

z_1 accommodation (size and comfort of seating, etc.)

z_2 ride qualities

z_3 handling and steering

z_4 engine (quietness and performance)

z_5 brakes

z_6 frequency of repair record (based on model of previous year)

z_S manufacturer's suggested retail price

The test reports are adjectival ("excellent," "good," "above average," "quiet," "severe brake fading," and so on) and were converted into

---

[1] We should distinguish clearly between Consumers Union's rating of automobiles with respect to particular properties (which we have taken as our characteristics here) and something quite different, its *overall rating* of the various models. Rating with respect to particular properties is merely a technical matter, although with a touch of judgment in some cases. It is not unreasonable to assume, however, that whether a car had good or poor engine performance is something that would be agreed upon objectively both by test drivers' comments and by objective performance measures. Having assessed the various models with respect to individual characteristics, Consumers Union then proceeds to use its own preferences as to what mix of characteristics it considers desirable. It is on this basis that it decides to rank one model higher on an "overall" rating scale than another. If, however, a substantial number of consumers prefer their mix different from that of Consumers Union, they may buy more of a model which is low on the Consumers Union ranking than of one which is high. In our analysis we use *only* the ratings with respect to individual characteristics. It is contrary to the whole spirit of the analysis to presume to choose the consumers' actual preferences.

Table 10.1   Characteristics of 1969 Model Automobiles, United States

Model	Ranking in terms of characteristics*						
	z_1	z_2	z_3	z_4	z_5	z_6	$z_\$$
Group I Compacts							
Valiant	3	3	4	2	1	4	1
Nova	2	1	3	3	3	1	3
Rambler	1	2	2	1	3	2	4
Falcon	2	2	1	4	2	3	2
Group II Intermediates							
Coronet	3	3	1	3	4	3	3
Fairlane	4	2	3	5	2	6	6
Rebel	5	1	2	2	1	5	5
Chevelle	2	2	6	1	4	1	7
Cutlass	1	1	5	4	3	4	1
Buick Special	2	1	4	4	3	3	2
Tempest	2	1	6	4	4	2	4
Group III Full-size, low-priced models only							
Ford	6	3	3	1	3	5	5
Biscayne	2	2	5	4	2	1	6
Catalina	3	2	6	5	5	6	1
Polara	5	4	4	2	4	2	2
Fury	4	1	1	2	4	3	4
Ambassador	1	2	2	3	1	4	3
Group IV All full-size							
Ford	10	4	4	1	3	5	8
Biscayne	4	3	7	4	2	1	9
Catalina	5	3	10	6	6	7	4
Polara	8	5	6	2	4	2	5
Fury	7	2	1	2	4	3	7
Ambassador	3	3	3	3	1	4	6
Executive	2	8	9	6	5	8	2
LeSabre	2	9	7	7	5	8	3
Newport	9	7	5	2	6	1	1
Monterey	6	6	2	5	4	6	3
Delta 88	1	1	8	7	4	7	3

* A higher figure implies more of the characteristic, price appearing inversely. Higher figure means lower price.

rankings on an ad hoc basis. "Marks" were assigned to give the rank orderings, a higher number for more of the characteristic. Since the test comments involve implicit reference to cars of the same general class, the analysis is carried out separately for each of four groups:

Group I   4 compact cars
Group II   7 intermediate cars
Group III   6 low-priced full-size cars
Group IV   11 full-size cars, including those of Group III

The characteristics "marks" for each of the groups are given in Table 10.1. Note that a higher mark for $ represents a lower price, and that the marks cannot be compared among different groups.

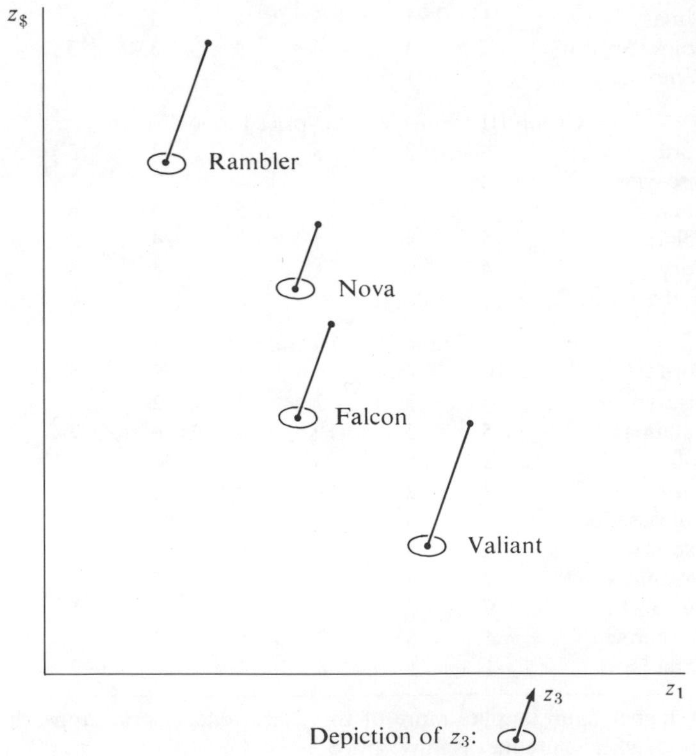

Figure 10.13. Group I. Compact cars

Analysis of all the pairwise combinations reveals the following:

(1) For group I (compacts), characteristics 1 (accommodation) and $ (price) were nearly sufficient to give the efficiency frontier, but characteristic 6 was necessary to give complete discrimination. The results are illustrated in Figure 10.13, where z_1 and $z_\$$ are on the plane and z_6 is represented by the height of the "posts," Thus it would seem that only three relevant characteristics are necessary for the analysis of this group of 4 cars.

(2) For group III (low-priced full-size), the above set of characteristics (1, $, 6) do not fully discriminate. The inclusion of characteristic 4 (engine) completes a set of 4 relevant characteristics sufficient to "explain" the market for 6 cars. The efficiency frontier in all four relevant characteristics is illustrated in Figure 10.14, using two "poles" for each point.

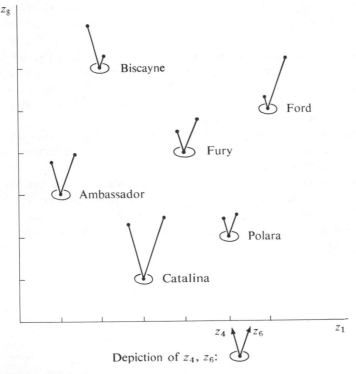

Figure 10.14. Group III

(3) For group IV (all full-size cars, including the group III models) all 110 pairwise comparisons reveal no dominance of one model by another when we use characteristics 1, 3, 4, 6, $. This gives five relevant characteristics for a group of 11 cars, and these characteristics include all those found relevant in group I and III.

(4) Results are slightly less clearcut for group II (intermediates). This group is fully "explained" by characteristics 1, 2, 3, 6, $—five relevant characteristics for 7 cars—but these are a somewhat different set of characteristics from those found for group IV. If we take the set found relevant for IV, which includes all those found relevant for I and III as well, we explain everything except a single comparison. With this set of characteristics, the Dodge Coronet dominates the Pontiac Tempest, but perhaps it is better to hypothesize that the same set of characteristics should apply to all groups, and live with the one comparison that suggests dominance.

Taken together, the analysis strongly supports both the hypothesis that markets can be explained with fewer characteristics than goods, and the usefulness of the revealed relevance technique. Only five of seven characteristics initially chosen seem relevant, and these five seem adequate to cover a total of 22 car models in four groups. Of special significance is the fact that the relevant set chosen for groups I and III independently contained the same characteristics that were also found relevant for the largest group, IV.

Our analysis suggests that the automobile market is readily amenable to rational analysis in terms of straightforward physical characteristics of cars, without using such imponderables as "style" or any sex at all. The relevant characteristics seem to be accommodation, handling and steering, engine, repair record, price. Ride quality and brakes do not seem to emerge as important relevant characteristics. Contrary to some mythology, there was no evidence of any car which was worse in all physical characteristics than some other, yet was able to sell at a higher price.

INDEX